MOUNT RUSHMORE

MONUMENT TO AMERICA'S DEMOCRACY

BY DOROTHY K. HILBURN & STEVEN L. WALKER

Above: The American symbol of freedom, the bald eagle, *Haliaeetus leucocephalus*, soaring through the blue skies of South Dakota. Bald eagles may have wing spans well over 6 feet.
PHOTO BY LEN RUE, JR.

Special thanks to James G. Popovich, Chief of Interpretation and Visitors Service, Mount Rushmore National Memorial, for his assistance in the creation of this book.

Left: Park Service workers Bob Crisman and Karl Bachman descend carving of Thomas Jefferson during inspection of cracks in Mount Rushmore.
PHOTO BY PAUL HORSTED

Front cover: The faces of American Presidents George Washington, Thomas Jefferson, Theodore Roosevelt and Abraham Lincoln gaze from the face of Mount Rushmore at the Mount Rushmore National Memorial in South Dakota.
PHOTO BY RUSS FINLEY

Cover background: Detail of the field of stars on Old Glory, the American Flag.
PHOTO BY KAREN SHELL

Below: Mount Rushmore's four regal presidents gaze out over the steep talus slope created by 450,000 tons of granite blasted off the cliff.
PHOTO BY RUSS FINLEY

Designed by Camelback Design Group, Inc., 8655 East Via de Ventura, Suite G200, Scottsdale, Arizona 85258. Phone: 602-948-4233. Distributed by Canyonlands Publications, 4860 North Ken Morey Drive, Bellemont, Arizona 86015. For ordering information please call (520) 779-3888.

Requests for additional information should be made to: Camelback/Canyonlands Venture at the address above, or call our toll free telephone number: 1-800-283-1983.

Library of Congress Catalog Number: 97-66358
International Standard Book Number: 1-879924-31-5

Proudly printed and bound in the USA.

INTRODUCTION...

Nestled deep within the heartland of the North American continent, in the Black Hills of South Dakota, rises a shrine of democracy featuring the regal countenances of four of America's greatest presidents: George Washington, commander of the Revolutionary Army and the first president; Thomas Jefferson, the author of the Declaration of Independence and third president; Abraham Lincoln, who freed the slaves and held the nation together through the Civil War as the 16th President; and the 26th president, Theodore Roosevelt, who was the driving force behind the Panama Canal, an early conservationist and the first president to stand up to big business by advocating the elimination of monopolies.

Created by the hand of nature, but shaped by the hand of man, the story of Mount Rushmore symbolizes the struggle of the American nation and its triumphs through the determination and ability of its leaders.

During the early 1920s, Doane Robinson, the secretary of the State Historical Society of South Dakota, believed that the future success of his state depended upon more than its agricultural base. He knew that the wonders of the Black Hills, with their majestic granite peaks, lush dark forests and cool riparian areas could offer a solution.

After reading of a mountain carving project in Atlanta, Georgia, Robinson contacted its sculptor, Gutzon Borglum, about the possibility of such a project in the Black Hills. Borglum responded with enthusiasm and in just a few years the carving of Mount Rushmore began.

It has been said that without any one of several components Mount Rushmore would never have been started, much less completed. This is absolutely true of Gutzon Borglum, for he was a visionary with the ability to create a carving of mountainous proportions. It is impossible to tell if any other artist would have had the ability to nudge, cajole and force the project, through its many ups and downs, to completion. The work he'd done on Stone Mountain, a mountain carving project he had been involved with in Atlanta, Georgia, helped him become an artist with the engineering needed for an endeavor of such a magnitude. He was a man with a personality as big as Mount Rushmore, and because of this he was able to create a public awareness of the project that led to the success of Mount Rushmore.

Borglum, the son of Danish immigrants, was a fiercely patriotic man who believed in the greatness of America. He believed American artists should create art matching the scope of America's greatness, and that anything less than that was something to be ashamed of. When Robinson first approached Borglum his idea was to carve an image of Red Cloud, a famous Sioux chief, or famous explorers like Lewis and Clark. But Borglum had a different idea. He wanted to create a memorial honoring

Left: George Washington, the first American president and father of the country, was sculptor Gutzon Borglum's first choice for the memorial and the first carving started on Mount Rushmore. The distance from top of Washington's head to the bottom of his chin is 60 feet.
PHOTO BY GARY LADD

Right: Clouds and ponderosa pine frame the four faces of George Washington, Thomas Jefferson, Theodore Roosevelt and Abraham Lincoln.
PHOTO BY RUSS FINLEY

the distinguished American presidents whose actions had created the greatest country in the world, the United States of America.

George Washington was represented because he was universally thought of as the father of the country. Thomas Jefferson was represented because he was the author of the Declaration of Independence and the person responsible for the Louisiana Purchase, which more than doubled the size of the country. Abraham Lincoln, a favorite subject of Borglum's, was included because he preserved the nation in its darkest hours and stood fast for human rights.

The selection of Theodore Roosevelt was the most controversial. Many believed Roosevelt's accomplishments were far too contemporary and had yet to stand the test of time. Borglum was a supporter of Roosevelt and believed that Roosevelt, by building the Panama Canal, had completed Columbus' dream of an easier route to the west. History, and the massive figures carved in the stone, show that Gutzon Borglum had his way.

Although there was serious opposition to

the project by people all over the country, the politicians of South Dakota saw the viability of such an undertaking and most supported the carving idea. Senator Peter Norbeck and Congressman William Williamson were both staunch supporters of Mount Rushmore and without their help it is entirely possible that the project would never have been completed.

They were able to secure desperately needed government funding that paid for most of the Mount Rushmore National Memorial project.

The project, which officially began October 4, 1927, and ended on October 31, 1941, took more than 14 years to complete, although only 6 1/2 years were actually spent carving. The cost was $989,992.32, of which $836,000 was paid for by the government.

Today, a price tag of less than one million dollars seems very inexpensive for this great memorial to America's democracy which is visited by more than 2.5 million people a year.

Below: Ponderosa pine, *Pinus ponderosa*, and the granite faces of Mount Rushmore.
PHOTO BY JEFF GNASS

A Geography of Mount Rushmore...

Geography... American Heritage Dictionary defines geography as: 1. "The study of the earth and its features and the distribution of life on the earth, including human life and the effects of human activity. 2. The geographic characteristics of an area. 3. A book on geography. 4. An ordered arrangement of constituent elements."

Mount Rushmore National Memorial is nestled among the ponderosa pine forests of the Black Hills in the southwest corner of South Dakota,

Location, Location, Location...

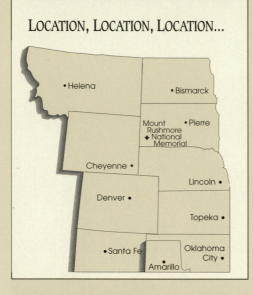

The Weather Forecast...

The chart below shows average monthly temperatures, precipitation and snowfall in Rapid City, 25 miles northeast of Mount Rushmore. Weather may vary greatly in different areas of this region due to variations in elevation and exposure. The Black Hills averages annual precipitation of 22 inches and thunderstorms, often accompanied by hail, are common in the summer months. Winter snowfall in the Black Hills averages from 60 to 100 inches.

Month	Average Maximum	Average Minimum	Extreme High	Extreme Low	Normal Precipitation	Normal Snowfall
January	33°	10°	77°	-28°	0.4	5
February	38°	15°	75°	-34°	0.5	7
March	45°	21°	81°	-18°	1.0	9
April	58°	32°	93°	1°	1.8	7
May	69°	43°	98°	18°	2.7	1
June	78°	52°	107°	31°	3.0	trace
July	98°	59°	110°	39°	1.9	0
August	86°	57°	107°	38°	1.6	0
September	75°	46°	104°	18°	1.2	trace
October	63°	37°	94°	10°	0.9	2
November	48°	22°	79°	-19°	0.6	5
December	38°	13°	75°	-30°	0.4	5

All temperatures above are in degrees Fahrenheit. Precipitation and snowfall are stated in inches.

The mean annual temperature of the Black Hills is 45.6° F. Spring weather varies; summer is warm with afternoon thunderstorms; fall is clear and mild with colors beginning to change in September.

Source: Data summaries compiled by USA Today Weather Almanac.

very close to the center of the North American continent. Rapid City, 25 miles northeast of the memorial, is the closest major city. The state capital of South Dakota is Pierre which is 196 miles northeast of Mount Rushmore.

The highest point in the Black Hills is Harney Peak at 7242 feet above sea level, while the highest point on Mount Rushmore is 5725 ft.

The memorial is open 24 hours a day, 7 days a week, all year long, although the orientation center and food/gift shops have separate hours. Mount Rushmore National Memorial is lighted every night of the year, with summer hours beginning at 9 p.m.

Camping and climbing are both prohibited on the faces of the memorial, although the Black Hills has other areas open to these past times.

A Hop, Skip, and a Jump...

Distances from Mount Rushmore National Memorial to other popular United States destinations by automobile:

Destination	Miles	Kilometers
Badlands NP	90	145
Chicago, IL	938	1509
Denver, CO	429	690
De Smet, SD	340	547
Devil's Tower NM	125	201
Glacier NP	1058	1702
Little Bighorn BNM	331	532
Minneapolis, MN	605	973
San Francisco, CA	1429	2299
Scottsbluff NM	199	320
Sioux Falls, SD	366	588
Yellowstone NP	406	653

Left: An aerial view of the Black Hills and Mount Rushmore National Memorial, South Dakota.
PHOTO BY RUSS FINLEY

For a more accurate picture of the weather patterns of the Black Hills, it is helpful to divide the Hills into 2 separate climactic zones, the Northern and Southern Hills areas.

DIMENSIONS...

Listed below are sizes of the president's features on Mount Rushmore and how they stack up to some famous landmarks from around the country and the world.

PRESIDENTIAL MEASUREMENTS:

Head	60 feet tall
Eye	11 feet wide
Nose	20 feet tall
Mouth	18 feet wide

SIZE OF FIGURES IF COMPLETED TO SCALE: 450 feet tall

COMPARED TO:

Washington Monument	555 feet tall
St. Louis Arch	630 feet tall
Statue of Liberty	151 feet tall
Eiffel Tower	1056 feet tall

It is easiest to differentiate between these zones by imagining a dividing line beginning at Rapid City and running due west through the Black Hills. The northern Hills have slightly cooler temperatures than the southern Hills.

MOUNT RUSHMORE...

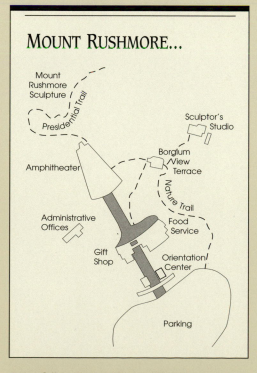

Snowfall in the northern Hills averages over 100 inches in the highest elevations, with a maximum recorded snowfall of 191.5, while the southern hills average much less.

Precipitation averages about 29 inches per year in the north and about 19 inches in the south. The lowest temperature ever recorded in the Black Hills was -52° at Custer, with the highest temperature ever recorded, 112° at Belle Fourche. The mean daily high temperatures average around the 50 to 60 degree range with the mean low temperatures averaging between 25 to 35 degrees.

Extreme weather conditions are not uncommon in the Black Hills area, with high winds often occurring in the spring and fall, and thunderstorms and hailstorms often occurring in the summers.

While weather in this area is not as severe as in other mountainous areas, it is wise to check weather conditions before starting a trip across the Hills and surrounding prairies.

DISTANCES TO OTHER ATTRACTIONS...

Mileages from the Mount Rushmore National Memorial to destinations within and around the Black Hills National Forest by automobile are as follows:

DESTINATION	MILES	DESTINATION	MILES	DESTINATION	MILES
1. Crazy Horse Memorial	17	3. Custer State Park	10	6. Hot Springs	49
2. Custer	20	4. Deadwood	52	7. Jewel Cave NM	31
		5. Harney Peak	12	8. Keystone	3
				9. Lead	53
				10. Spearfish	70
				11. Sturgis	53
				12. Wind Cave NP	30

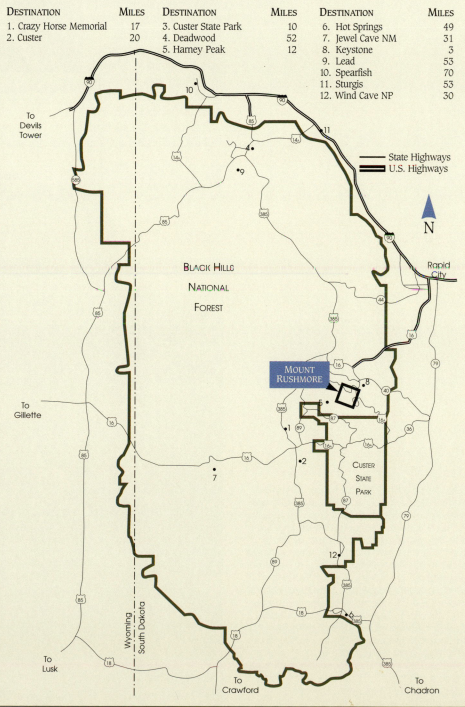

THE MEN WHO MADE IT HAPPEN...

While sculptor Gutzon Borglum was able to carve a granite mountain in the Black Hills of South Dakota into the colossal memorial we see today, this great achievement would never have been possible without the collective strength and resources of several men whose dedication to the concept of a memorial carving on Mount Rushmore was unwavering.

Without the efforts of Doane Robinson Mount Rushmore's memorial would never have been created. A South Dakota lawyer whose real name, Jonah Leroy Robinson, was seldom used, Doane Robinson was born in Sparta, Wisconsin on the 19th of October in 1856. Called Doane by all from a very early age, Robinson became a Dakota Territory lawyer

Doane Robinson.
PHOTO: MILLER STUDIO

sometime in the 1880s. An educated, articulate and witty man, he eventually left the practice of law to become a poet and speaker whose works appeared in many leading magazines of the day including *Century*, *McClure's* and *Arena*. In 1901, Robinson, who had become known far and wide as the "Dakota Poet and Humorist," became the first secretary of the State Historical Society of South Dakota.

In his capacity as the secretary of the State Historical Society, Robinson believed South Dakota needed greater sources of revenue from tourism. He, along with the rest of the country, had witnessed the publicity surrounding Stone Mountain in Atlanta in the early 1920s and decided the granite peaks of South Dakota's Black Hills would be an excellent location for a mountain carving.

Before attempting to contact a sculptor for the project, Robinson sought the support of Senator Peter Norbeck. Norbeck, a self-made man who had found considerable success by developing

Right: On July 17, 1929, the Mount Rushmore National Memorial Commission met at Mount Rushmore. Present were, front from left to right: John A. Boland of Rapid City, South Dakota; Julius Rosenwald, board chairman of Sears, Roebuck & Company, of Chicago, Illinois; Doane Robinson of Pierre, South Dakota; the sculptor, Gutzon Borglum (in hat); William Williamson of Custer, South Dakota; Frank Lowden of Oregon, Illinois; Fred W. Sargent, president of Chicago & Northwestern Railway, of Chicago, Illinois; Royal C. Johnson of Aberdeen, South Dakota; and Lorine J. Spoonts of Corpus Christi, Texas. In the rear, from left to right: Delos B. Gurney of Yankton, South Dakota; Joseph S. Cullinan, president of Texaco, of Houston, Texas; Charles M. Day of Sioux Falls, South Dakota.
PHOTO COURTESY NATIONAL PARK SERVICE

Senator Peter Norbeck was an early conservationist who created Custer State Park and helped preserve Grand Teton and Yellowstone.
PHOTOGRAPHER UNKNOWN

an inexpensive method of water well-drilling, was born in 1870 to Swedish immigrants. Senator Norbeck had a deep love of nature and was directly responsible for the creation of a 75,000 acre game preserve in the Black Hills known as Custer State Park Game Sanctuary, later to become Custer State Park. His love of the outdoors drove him to push for legislation conserving many of America's natural areas including Badlands National Park, Grand Teton National Park and additional lands around Yellowstone. Norbeck is responsible for the design of the Needles Highway and the Iron Mountain Road, the beautiful scenic route over Iron Mountain famous for its tunnels which frame Mount Rushmore. In addition to his love of nature, Norbeck had a deep affection for art.

Senator Norbeck realized the potential for South Dakota tourism that a massive carving could create and decided to help Robinson attain support for the creation of a mountain carving in the Black Hills.

Robinson then announced his concept of a colossal mountain carving to the people of South Dakota, an idea that quickly generated a considerable amount of controversy. Many believed no human should dare desecrate mountains that had been formed by the hands of God, while others felt Robinson's idea was a practical solution for bringing much needed tourist dollars to the state.

Doane Robinson first contacted noted sculptor Lorado Taft with an idea to carve an image of Red Cloud, the famous Sioux chief, or perhaps the images of explorers Lewis and Clark. Taft's health precluded his participation in the idea so Robinson decided to contact the creator of the controversial Stone Mountain– a massive undertaking just outside Atlanta, Georgia (see sidebar page 15)– John Gutzon de la Mothe Borglum. When Gutzon Borglum responded

Artist Gutzon Borglum hangs from a bosun's chair on the face of Mount Rushmore.
PHOTO: RISE STUDIO (1930)

to his letter, Robinson was filled with hope that his dream might come true.

Gutzon Borglum traveled to South Dakota in September of 1924 to meet with Robinson and to survey the Black Hills for a possible carving site. He found the area to be filled with possibilities and thought that the Mount Harney area might be the perfect location for a mountain carving.

When Senator Norbeck met Gutzon Borglum in December of 1924, his love and knowledge of art impressed Borglum, while Borglum's talent and passion inspired Senator Norbeck. Norbeck's confidence in Borglum's ability made

William Williamson.
PHOTO: MILLER STUDIO

him feel comfortable enough to approach his friend, Congressman William Williamson, for legislative support of the carving idea.

Rep. Williamson and Senator Norbeck were long time friends who had great respect for each other. Williamson, like Norbeck, was of Scandinavian decent and had grown up in central South Dakota. Williamson was a hard

HOW MOUNT RUSHMORE WAS NAMED...

When attorney Charles E. Rushmore was sent to South Dakota by his New York employer to inquire about cassiterite mines near the town of Keystone, no one had any idea that his name would become associated with one of America's greatest national treasures.

In the 1870s and 1880s the Black Hills were a hot bed of mining activity. Although the Black Hills rightfully belonged to the Sioux, who had been granted the land in and around the Black Hills in the Treaty of 1868, the miners who poured into the area around 1876 showed no concern about land ownership, they were only interested in finding gold.

Gold was first discovered near Harney Peak in 1874 and when news of the discovery rang across the country, miners hoping to strike it rich headed for the Hills. While most of the miners were disappointed with mining, some actually made significant claims. The Black Hills are the home of the largest North American producer of gold, the Homestake Mining Company. Discovered in 1874, the Homestake is still the largest supplier of gold in North America.

Gold was not the only mineral of value to be found in the Hills. The hard silicate, beryl, and tourmaline, a mineral that is often valuable when transparent, were also found in the Hills. Mica; spodumene; amblygonite, an important source of lithium; and a dark mineral called cassiterite, which is the chief source of metallic tin, were also discovered in the area. It was in the interest of tin that young Rushmore first came to the Black Hills.

During his several trips to the area in 1884 and 1885 to secure options on several cassiterite locations, as well as the Etta Mine, the personable young attorney earned the respect and affection of the prospectors, miners and guides with whom he lived in a log cabin camp during his frequent stays. Rushmore's interest in one particularly impressive granite mountain was rewarded when he inquired about its name. "Never had any, but it has now– we'll call the damn thing Rushmore," came the reply from his guide. It took 45 years for the name to be

finally be officially recognized by the United States Board of Geographic Names, despite the fact that it had always been referred to as either Mt. Rushmore or Rushmore Peak since the late 1800s.

Charles E. Rushmore left South Dakota and returned to New York to continue his career in the legal profession, and when the idea of producing

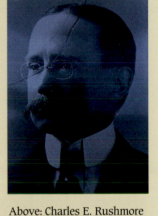

Above: Charles E. Rushmore was a 28 year old lawyer visiting South Dakota from New York on business when locals decided to name a granite mountain after him.
COURTESY NATIONAL PARK SERVICE

a mountain carving on "his" mountain had become more than a just a possibility, Rushmore donated $5000 of his own funds, a major sum at that time, to the Mount Rushmore project.

Although Charles E. Rushmore did little more than ride by the mountain and inquire into its name, history still had a hand in remembering a New York City lawyer who was so well liked by the common people he visited, in the then very remote Black Hills of South Dakota, they named a mountain after him, and kept pressure on the United States Board of Geographic Names for 45 years to keep the man's name on their mountain.

Today, the mountain is known as the home of the impressive mountain carving which stands as a permanent memorial honoring four United States presidents. Although Gutzon Borglum, Doane Robinson and Senator Peter Norbeck had so much more to do with the success of the carving, it is Charles E. Rushmore whose name will go down in history.

worker who became a lawyer and was active in South Dakota politics from a young age. Williamson became a judge in 1911 and nine years later was elected to Congress.

Williamson introduced a bill requesting permission from the state to carve statues in Harney National Forest and on March 3, 1925, the bill became law. Although the idea now had legal permission, the project needed money to begin. Some money was raised by donations, but the problem of money would plague the Mount Rushmore project for many years to come. One thing is certain, without Williamson, the project may have never come to completion.

Williamson, and others, invited President Calvin Coolidge to spend the summer of 1927 in the Black Hills of South Dakota and when the president accepted, plans were made to garner his support for the Mount Rushmore project. Those plans worked and at the second

Calvin Coolidge, here in an Indian headdress, became the 30th president upon President Warren G. Harding's death.
COURTESY SOUTH DAKOTA SCHOOL OF MINING AND TECHNOLOGY

dedication of Mt. Rushmore President Coolidge addressed the crowds asking for more support for the project. His support was pivotal for the enterprise's success.

One of the most important people to become involved in Mount Rushmore was John A. Boland, a South Dakota business man who was an appointee to the Mount Rushmore Commission.

Boland's job was fund raiser and overseer of the project's finances. His was possibly the most difficult job of all.

It fell to Boland to

ensure payment of all expenditures and to determine if there was enough money to continue work on the mountain.

Because Boland took his job seriously, he often butted heads with Borglum. After several years of threats, Borglum was able to rid himself of John Boland in 1938 when a new commission granted Borglum control.

John A. Boland was dedicated to Mount Rushmore but found himself at odds with the sculptor, Gutzon Borglum, over control of project finances.
PHOTO: HARRIS & EWING

Right: Profile of George Washington, commander of the Revolutionary Army and first president of the United States of America.
PHOTO BY RUSS FINLEY

PRESIDENT COOLIDGE LENDS A HAND...

One very important component to the success of Mount Rushmore can be credited to the 30th U.S. president, Calvin Coolidge.

Born John Calvin Coolidge on July 4, 1872, in Plymouth, Vermont, Coolidge had come through the political ranks first as Mayor of Northampton, Massachusetts, then as a Senator, Lieutenant Governor, and Governor of Massachusetts before becoming Warren G. Harding's vice president.

Coolidge became president when Harding died unexpectedly during a cross-country trip. In an unusual turn of events, Coolidge's father, John Coolidge, a justice of the peace and notary public, performed the act of swearing his son into the office of the presidency.

Coolidge's affiliation with Mount Rushmore began in the summer of 1927. Members of the state of South Dakota had done their best to entice the president with images of a dry, mild, mosquito-less summer in the beautiful ponderosa pine forests of the Black Hills. Their efforts paid off, resulting in one of the best breaks ever for Mount Rushmore.

President and Mrs. Coolidge stayed at the Game Lodge in the Hills and enjoyed South Dakota so much that they extended their three week

President Calvin Coolidge at the 1927 dedication of Mount Rushmore. His support was a turning point in the continuation of the project.
PHOTO BY CHARLES D'EMERY

vacation to three months. One reason the visit was so successful was because of the healthful effect of the climate on the president. Coolidge's bronchitis had always been a problem but his doctor proclaimed: "the Black Hills are improving the health of President Coolidge."

During the summer, Calvin and Grace Coolidge seemed to become a part of the community. They attended a small church and spent time getting to know the area. The president was also honored when the state changed the name of one of the peaks in the Black Hills to "Mount Coolidge."

Never one to let an opportunity slip by, Gutzon Borglum flew over the Game Lodge in a small plane and tossed a floral wreath to the lodge's lawn with a note that read, "Greetings from Mount Rushmore to Mount Coolidge."

While Mrs. Coolidge enjoyed knitting and

The president learns to fish on June 16, 1927, in the Black Hills of South Dakota.
PHOTO COURTESY SOUTH DAKOTA SCHOOL OF MINING AND TECHNOLOGY

relaxing at the Game Lodge, the president went trout fishing– a past time that was new to him, and that was unusually successful. Of course, he had no way of knowing that the river he fished in had been secretly over stocked with fat trout hungry for any sign of bait.

The president had said at the beginning of his trip that he would make no formal appearances, but after much prodding, he changed his mind and on August 10, 1927, he put on a cowboy hat and chaps and rode a horse up the mountain for the second dedication of Mount Rushmore.

After his dedication speech Coolidge presented Borglum with a set of drills. A flag ceremony was performed while Borglum climbed to the top of the mountain and symbolically drilled the first holes into the mountain.

The president told the crowd that "...their effort and courage entitles them to the sympathy and support of private beneficence and of the national government." This was exactly the kind of endorsement the project needed. Coolidge also offered his speech to be sold for fund raising.

President Coolidge's early support was without a doubt a turning point in the Mount Rushmore project. His support influenced the government's decision to fund the memorial, without which the hopes and dreams of Doane Robinson, Peter Norbeck, Gutzon Borglum and many others would have perished, and America would never have never known the glory of this permanent Shrine of Democracy.

President Coolidge takes a wagon ride to visit Nebraska's ex-governor Samuel McKelvie at his Slate Creek Cabin.
COURTESY SOUTH DAKOTA SCHOOL OF MINING AND TECHNOLOGY

GEOLOGY OF THE BLACK HILLS...

The Black Hills of South Dakota and northeast Wyoming are among the oldest formations of granite exposed on the surface of the earth. The geologic composition of Mount

The massive Harney Peak Granite batholith in the center of the Black Hills has a diameter of approximately 9 miles and extends beneath the earth's surface to depths unknown. These ancient granite deposits were formed during the Proterozoic period of the Precambrian era, around 1.7 billion years ago, as magma from the earth's molten core thrust into layers of sediments from an ancient ocean. These sediments were compressed into deposits of sandstone, shale, limestone and siltstone of great depth, over a period of millions of years. As the magma intruded into the deposits, mica schist, a metamorphic rock formed by intense heat and pressure was created.

Periods of uplift, created as the earth's plates moved into each other, in a process called plate tectonics, uplifted the Rocky Mountains and the Black Hills. This moved the granite deposits closer to the surface. The last uplift is believed to have occurred around 60 million years ago during the Paleocene period of the Cenozoic era. Continual

exposure to the forces of erosion– water, wind, frost wedging, chemical and organic weathering– removed the less resistant layer of sedimentary and metamorphic deposits to expose

Above: The Cathedral Spires in Custer State Park.
PHOTO BY PAUL HORSTED

Rushmore is composed of Harney Peak granite, pegmatite, the large grained white colored streaks across the George Washington and Abraham Lincoln faces and mica schist which can be seen below the area that represents Washington's waist and at Borglum View Terrace where it serves as a building material.

Above: Needles Eye in the Black Hills. The Needles were the first site suggested by Doane Robinson for a mountain carving by Borglum.   PHOTO BY JEFF GNASS

the granitic formations we find today.

Sculptor Gutzon Borglum was first directed to the Needles in Custer State Park as a potential site for the planned mountain carvings by Doane Robinson. Borglum considered the thin

Above: A National Park Service interpreter points out an example of boxwork, an unusual formation of thin calcite fins shaped like honeycombs, in Wind Cave National Park, also a part of the Black Hills uplift. PHOTO BY PAUL HORSTED

spires of the Needles, the quality of their granite was suitable, but did not offer the mass he

envisioned for his epic project. He returned from his first trip to the Black Hills without finding a suitable site. A year later, in August of 1925, he returned and chose Mount Rushmore over other Black Hills formations because its granite deposits were of a finer grain than others in the area.

While he carved Mount Rushmore Borglum had to frequently change his design to fit the geology of the mountain. The Jefferson face was originally planned for the right of Washington but had to be removed when uncarvable schist was encountered. The Washington figure needed twenty feet of surface rock removed before the proper carving surface was found. The Jefferson and Lincoln figures were some sixty feet inside Mount Rushmore waiting to be released by the sculptor and Theodore Roosevelt was between and 100 and 120 feet inside the granite formation.

The hard granite of Mount Rushmore will be slow to erode, estimates are as low as one inch each 10,000 years. The greatest dangers to Mount Rushmore are from frost wedging and surface expansion which form cracks. Borglum was aware of this potential problem and sealed

the carvings with a mixture of linseed oil, granite dust and white lead to prevent water seepage. Today, a high grade silicone caulk is administered regularly to treat cracks as part of the Park Service's maintenance program.

Above: The Black Hills are also home to Jewel Cave National Monument, the fourth longest cave in the world. Jewel Cave is named for the sparkle of the calcite features lining its walls. There is current speculation that Jewel Cave and Wind Cave may be connected underground.
PHOTO BY PAUL HORSTED

Below: Eroded Black Hills granite formations in Custer State Park, South Dakota.
PHOTO BY DICK DIETRICH

THE MAN WHO CARVED A MOUNTAIN...

It took a man of strength, vision, talent and fierce determination to design and create the massive memorial that would become known as the "Shrine of Democracy," Mount Rushmore National Memorial. John Gutzon de la Mothe Borglum was just such a man.

Although the idea of carving figures into the granite mountains of the Black Hills was originally conceived by South Dakota lawyer and poet, Doane Robinson, the man who would become famous for designing and creating the massive mountain carvings was a man unlike any other.

Gutzon Borglum in 1934.
PHOTO BY CHARLES D'EMERY

In 1864, 25 year old Jens Borglum left Denmark and crossed the Atlantic Ocean to travel to the Mormon mecca, Salt Lake City. En route he met and married Ida Mikkelsen. Within a few years of their marriage, Ida's younger sister Christina came to Utah and Jens, following Mormon tradition, married her as well. The Borglum family, Jen, Ida and Christine moved to Idaho where Christina gave birth to John Gutzon de la Mothe Borglum on March 25, 1867. Christina gave birth to another son, Solon Hannibal, on December 22, 1868 and in June of the following year Ida gave birth to a boy named Arnold.

In 1869, for one reason or another, the Borglum family experienced a split. Christina left the family and later remarried. Her children were raised by Jens and Ida who moved to St. Louis where Jens studied to become a doctor. Upon graduation, he changed his name to James and moved the family to Fremont, Nebraska, where he became a general practitioner.

Even as a young boy Gutzon showed artistic talent and when he was in his teens he went to California where he began to seriously study art. Borglum studied painting and in 1889, when he was only 22 years old, he married his 40 year old painting instructor, Elizabeth Jaynes Putnam. Liza, as she was often called, was a prominent artist in her own right and after their marriage took young Borglum's career in hand.

In 1890, Liza and Gutzon moved to Paris where Borglum became a student of the Julian Academy and the Ecole des Beaux-Arts. It was during this time in Paris that Borglum first began to sculpt. He became acquainted with, and studied under, the famous French artist Auguste René Rodin, whose artistic genius greatly affected the young Borglum. Liza and Gutzon also traveled to Spain and England where his exhibit even caught the discerning eye of Queen Victoria.

Gutzon's brother, Solon, studied sculpting at the Cincinnati Art Academy and he quickly achieved a large measure of success. Later, Solon went to Paris where his reputation as a gifted sculptor was reinforced by approval of the Paris art society. Solon's success seemed to spur Gutzon into making a change from painting to sculpting.

After 12 years of marriage, Borglum left Liza in Paris and moved to New York City. Shortly after setting up an art studio he became seriously ill with typhoid fever. Liza hurried to America to offer care to her estranged husband and instead of finding her husband awaiting

In 1911 Gutzon Borglum created this giant statue of President Lincoln for the Newark, New Jersey Courthouse grounds.
PHOTO: CHARLES D'EMERY

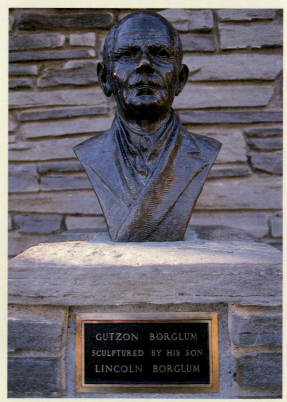

GUTZON BORGLUM
SCULPTURED BY HIS SON
LINCOLN BORGLUM

Right: Gutzon Borglum's son, Lincoln, worked closely with his father on Mount Rushmore and later became a sculptor. This bust of his father is one of Lincoln Borglum's works.
PHOTO COURTESY NATIONAL PARK SERVICE

her care, she discovered another woman, Mary Montgomery, nursing Borglum back to health. Gutzon and Liza later divorced.

Borglum had met Mary Montgomery on the ship that carried him away from both France and Liza. In 1909, he married the diminutive Miss Montgomery, a young, intelligent woman who had acted as his secretary for several years. Marriage to Mary proved to be a steadying influence on the excitable artist.

In the years before his marriage to Mary, Borglum created several outstanding art pieces including both murals and statuettes. He was honored by inclusion in the membership ranks of the National Sculpture Society, of which Solon Borglum was also a member. In what became the lifelong pattern of his behavior, an altercation between Gutzon and the society occurred and, shortly before the society could revoke his membership, he resigned.

Gutzon Borglum and his son, Lincoln, ride a tram car to the top of Mount Rushmore.
PHOTO: CHARLES D'EMERY

Sculpting became Borglum's main form of artistic expression and his talent led to the honor of a gold medal at the 1904 St. Louis Exposition. Winning the gold medal led to many opportunities for Borglum including a commission to complete a large number of statues for the Cathedral of St. John the Divine in New York, a bust of Abraham Lincoln which can still be seen in the Rotunda of the Capital Building, a wonderfully beautiful work featuring horses called Mares of Diomedes, a remodeling of the Statue of Liberty's torch and a large bust of Theodore Roosevelt. Borglum also created a statue of General Philip Sheridan atop his horse which was placed in Sheridan Park in Washington D.C. Borglum's works can be found in many countries around the world including Cuba, Denmark, France and England.

A man of great energy and enthusiasm,

On October 1, 1925 Borglum raised the flag on the summit of Mount Rushmore at the mountain's dedication ceremony.
PHOTO: CHARLES D'EMERY

Borglum became an unqualified success as a sculptor whose talent was recognized in both Europe and America. Borglum was the type of man who inspired either deep loyalty or fierce resentment. His brash personality and penchant for stirring up controversy and his frequent habit of using the media to air his complaints all contributed to his reputation as being difficult to work with, along with making him many enemies.

Borglum sculpting an early Mount Rushmore model.
PHOTO BY CHARLES D'EMERY

On the other hand, Borglum could also be charming, gentle and kind. He had a very charismatic personality and was an eloquent speaker who, if he so chose, could convert even his staunchest opponents to his way of thinking. These finer qualities enabled him to make lasting friends.

THE STONE MOUNTAIN CONTROVERSY...

A Georgia newspaper man by the name of Jack T. Graves has been credited with being the first to propose the carving of a monument on Stone Mountain. His idea appeared as an editorial in 1915 but it took Mrs. Helen Plane, a Civil War widow, to act as a catalyst in bringing the idea to sculptor Gutzon Borglum.

Mrs. Plane was the president of the United Daughters of the Confederacy and she believed a great monument to the South could, and should, be formed in the steep granite walls of Stone Mountain east of Atlanta.

Stone Mountain is believed to be the world's largest body of exposed granite, consisting of some 7,532,750,950 cubic feet, or 583 acres, of granite. Millions of cubic feet have already been quarried and Stone Mountain granite can be found on buildings throughout the world as well as in the lining of the Panama Canal.

When Borglum, who had long believed that American artists should create large American art, looked at the 3000 by 800 foot face of Stone Mountain he was immediately interested in the project. He envisioned a glorious scene of marching soldiers pulling heavy artillery and being led by several famous Confederate leaders including General Robert E. Lee and the beloved Stonewall Jackson.

Those who had brought Borglum to Atlanta loved his ideas and commissioned him to do the job. A dedication took place in 1916 but unfortunately, World War I interfered with the work until 1922, when work began in earnest.

Borglum and his team of workers spent much time overcoming the difficulties of working on such a large surface. It was his experience with Stone Mountain that made it possible for him to know how to proceed on the Mount Rushmore project. In January of 1924, a ceremony unveiling the carved head of Lee took place. Those who had served under Lee in the Civil War were moved to comment on how much the carving

Model of Gutzon Borglum's vision for the Stone Mountain carving. When Borglum discovered that he was about to be fired, he returned to his studio and destroyed all models.
PHOTO COURTESY NATIONAL PARK SERVICE

actually looked like the great general.

Soon after the unveiling, hostility over control of the project broke out between Borglum and the administrators of the Stone Mountain Monumental Association. The association believed that Borglum spent too much time away from the mountain on other projects, including a trip to Mount Rushmore, while Borglum accused the association of being too lax in fund raising, and wasting, or stealing, the money that was raised for the project. National public opinion sided with Borglum with the consensus being that Borglum should not have been bothered with "miserable money matters" and that he should be allowed the artistic freedom so necessary for a man of his talents.

When Borglum discovered the association was going to fire him he destroyed his models of Stone Mountain, which so angered the association that they tried to have him arrested. When all was said and done, Borglum was dismissed but not arrested.

Although there were hard feelings between Borglum and the association, he later considered going back to Atlanta to finish the job. In 1964, Massachusetts sculptor Walker Hancock was commissioned to finish the memorial, which was finally completed in 1970.

Gutzon Borglum was a man who frequently shot from the hip with little thought of the consequences his words may have. It is quite possible that his outspokenness prevented him from attaining even greater acclaim as an artist during his lifetime.

In contrast, Gutzon's brother Solon continued in his quiet way to build a body of work that placed him in a category that was at the time thought to be far more prestigious than that of Gutzon. In 1911, Solon was listed in the Encyclopedia Brittanica and Gutzon was only briefly mentioned in his biography.

Gutzon Borglum stands on a scaffold and directs detail work on President Theodore Roosevelt's face.
PHOTO CHARLES D'EMERY

During his lifetime Gutzon's many interests led him in some unusual directions for an artist. Interested in aeronautics, Borglum was a member of the Aeronautical Club of America and was present during a few of the Wright brothers' earliest flights. This interest in flying led him to become involved, after the start of World War I and at his own expense, in an investigation of the American aircraft industry, which he felt was both corrupt and incompetent. Many of his suspicions were correct and his actions resulted in President Wilson's creation of a committee to further investigate the aircraft industry.

Borglum was a passionately patriotic man and actively campaigned for Theodore Roosevelt and several other politicians whose views he supported. Besides being political, he was a physically active man who believed in living life to the fullest. He enjoyed most sports,

particularly boxing and fencing. As a husband and father, he and Mary had a son, Lincoln and a daughter, Mary Ellis, Borglum was also quite passionate. His family went with him on many of his assignments and he was in the habit of taking his son Lincoln along wherever he went.

One thing was certain, Gutzon Borglum was surely man enough to tackle the oversized task of mountain carving. His mountain carving career began in 1915 when he went to Atlanta to meet several members of the United Daughters of the Confederacy to discuss a commission to carve a huge relief on Stone Mountain (see sidebar page 15).

Although it is not totally clear who first thought of carving a monument on Stone Mountain, Helen Plane, a Civil War widow, was the catalyst who brought the idea to Borglum. Mrs. Plane was the president of the United Daughters of the Confederacy and she believed that a great monument could be formed from of the huge granite walls of Stone Mountain.

Borglum looked at the 3000 foot long by 800 foot high face of Stone Mountain and soon envisioned a glorious scene of marching soldiers of Confederacy pulling heavy artillery while being led by several famous Confederate generals including the beloved figures of Robert E. Lee, riding

Sculptor Gutzon Borglum directs the gaze of President Franklin D. Roosevelt and governor Tom Berry of South Dakota to the memorial at the dedication of the Jefferson face.
BLACK HILLS STUDIO

his famous horse Traveller, and Thomas J. "Stonewall" Jackson, a Southern hero.

Those who'd brought Borglum to Atlanta loved his ideas and quickly commissioned him to undertake the project, with a dedication taking place in 1916. Unfortunately, World War I interfered with the project until 1922, when work began in earnest. Borglum and a team of helpers worked out the difficulties of working

Left: Borglum in a tram car in 1936. In the early years of the Mount Rushmore project the tram was not strong enough to carry more than one person at a time to the top of the mountain so workmen had to hike up the mountain and then climb 506 wooden stairs each day to show up on the job site and repeat the process to get back down again when the day's work was done.
PHOTO BY RISE STUDIO

on such a large surface and in January 1924, a ceremony took place to unveil the carved head of General Lee.

Soon after the unveiling, hostility broke out over the project finances. Those administering the funds felt Gutzon was not allocating the time necessary

Borglum, swinging from a bosun's chair, directs work on President Lincoln's face.
PHOTO BY CHARLES D'EMERY

at Stone Mountain site to keep the project on time and within budget. The Stone Mountain Association believed that Borglum spent too much time away from the mountain on other projects, including a trip to Mount Rushmore, while Borglum accused the association of being too lax in fund raising, and of wasting money that was raised for the project.

When Borglum discovered the association was going to fire him, he destroyed his models of Stone Mountain, which so angered the association that they tried to have Borglum arrested. When all was said and done, he was dismissed but not arrested. The project lapsed into near oblivion until 1964, when sculptor Walker Hancock was commissioned to finish the memorial, which he finally completed in 1970.

Surprisingly, Borglum's troubles in Georgia only slightly affected the South Dakota project.

Borglum worked on Mount Rushmore until his death on March 6, 1941. His son, Lincoln Borglum, worked on the project until October 31, 1941, when work on the carving officially ended. Gutzon Borglum has become famous for the creation of a mountain carving that honors and celebrates democracy. Borglum's commitment to Mount Rushmore was never doubted and it is believed that without his artistic creativity Mount Rushmore National Memorial may never have been completed.

Right: Four United States presidents– George Washington, Thomas Jefferson, Abraham Lincoln and Theodore Roosevelt– stare from the face of Mount Rushmore, the result of Gutzon Borglum's unrelenting drive and artistic genius.
PHOTO BY DICK DIETRICH

ART, ENGINEERING AND POLITICS...

When attorney Charles E. Rushmore was sent to South Dakota by his New York City employer to make inquires regarding cassiterite mines near the town of Keystone, no one had any idea how important the name Rushmore would become in American history.

Although the Black Hills of South Dakota rightfully belonged to the Sioux Indians, who had been granted the land in and around the Black Hills in the Treaty of 1868, the miners who poured into the area around 1876 showed no concern about land ownership, they were looking for gold. Gold was first discovered near Harney Peak in 1874 and when news of the discovery spread across the country, miners hoping to strike it rich headed for the Hills.

Some miners did strike it rich. The Black Hills are home to the largest North American producer of gold, the Homestake Mine. Discovered in 1874 by the Manuel brothers, who worked the claim with Henry Harney and Alex Engh until Harney and Engh later sold their share for $300. Fred Manuel continued to work the mine until millionaire George Hearst convinced him to sell out for $70,000. Today, the Homestake is still the largest supplier of gold in North America.

The Sioux, understandably angered by the influx of whites, attacked miners whenever possible but were eventually forced to give up the Black Hills, a matter still in dispute today, to the United States government. Small towns quickly appeared and miners found the area to be full of minerals. Besides gold other minerals such as the hard silicate, beryl, were found in the hills, as was tourmaline, a mineral that is often valuable when transparent; mica; spodumene; amblygonite, an important source of lithium, and a dark mineral called cassiterite which is the chief source of metallic tin. It was in the interest of tin that young Rushmore came to the Black Hills.

During his several trips to the area in 1884 and 1885, the personable young Rushmore earned the respect and affection of the prospectors, miners, guides and businessmen with whom he associated during his long stays. His interest in one particularly impressive granite mountain was rewarded when he inquired about its name, "Never had any, but it has now–we'll call the damn thing Rushmore," was the reply of his guide. Today, Mount Rushmore is known worldwide for its impressive carvings which stand as a permanent memorial honoring four United States presidents.

In the 1920s, across the country in Atlanta Georgia, a proposed mountain carving project at Stone Mountain was getting a great deal of publicity. The story reached South Dakota poet and humorist, Doane Robinson who, as secretary of the State Historical Society, believed the massive granite peaks in the Black Hills would be ideal for a mountain carving.

Left: Located in the beautiful Black Hills of South Dakota, Mount Rushmore National Memorial draws 2.5 million visitors every year.
PHOTO BY PAUL HORSTED

Right: This view of the memorial shows the talus slope created by the roughly 450,000 tons of rock blasted from the mountain.
PHOTO BY PAUL HORSTED

Robinson believed a major project such as a mountain carving would draw tourists, and their pocketbooks, to the state. He sought support for the project from other civic-minded citizens, including Senator Peter Norbeck of South Dakota, whose love of nature resulted in the creation of the Custer State Park in the Black Hills and preservation of Grand Teton and the Badlands National Parks.

Senator Norbeck was also responsible for the design of two of the most scenic drives in America, the Needles Highway and the Iron Mountain Road, famous for its tunnels which frame the faces of Mount Rushmore. Norbeck and state engineer Scovel Johnson used dynamite to blast through areas of the Black Hills in order to develop roads that would blend with the beautiful natural scenery of areas surrounding the route.

Twisty hairpin curves, wooden bridges and the almost impossibly narrow tunnels were constructed in such a way as to nearly force travelers to view the scenery and enjoy their trip through the Black Hills in a leisurely manner.

Driller "honeycombing" the granite face while suspended from an aerial cage. Honeycombing helped control depth of pieces being removed.
PHOTO BY LINCOLN BORGLUM

When Robinson approached Norbeck with the idea of a mountain carving Norbeck quickly realized the potential for tourism that such a carving could create and he decided to help Doane Robinson attain support for the idea of a mountain carving in the Black Hills.

Robinson contacted the creator of the Stone Mountain carving, a famous sculptor named Gutzon Borglum. A man of great vision, energy and enthusiasm, Borglum was a painter and a sculptor whose talent was recognized in both Europe and America. He was the type of man to inspire either deep loyalty or fierce resentment and his selection by Robinson was controversial right from the start.

Borglum's mountain carving career began in 1915 with Stone Mountain. Rising 1683 feet above sea level, Stone Mountain, believed to be between 285 and 294 million years old, is the world's largest body of exposed granite. The north side of the massive granite mountain

Right: National Park Service worker Bob Crisman descends the carving of Abraham Lincoln during an inspection of cracks at Mount Rushmore.
PHOTO BY PAUL HORSTED

was the chosen site for Borglum's memorial to the Confederacy but, after a fight with the Stone Mountain Association over finances, Borglum left the project, destroying his models, which ensured no other sculptor could finish the project using his designs. The Stone Mountain Memorial was finally completed by another artist in 1970.

History has proven Robinson right in his choice of artists, for Borglum was the right man for the project. He was a charming and charismatic man, when he wasn't being a temperamental artist. His enthusiasm and eloquent speech could convince even his staunchest opponents that his way of thinking was correct after all. Unfortunately, Borglum's bullheadedness could also help push people away. One thing is certain, he was a man who received attention

The Washington figure, shown here in 1930, was the first of the 60 foot faces to emerge from the rock.   PHOTO: RISE STUDIO

every where he went, especially from the news media. His strong personality and speaking

skills proved to be an advantage for the Mount Rushmore memorial project.

Borglum went to South Dakota in September,

1924, to meet with Robinson and to survey the Black Hills for a possible carving site. He found the area full of possibilities and thought the Mount Harney area was perfect for a mountain carving.

When Senator Norbeck met Borglum his confidence in the artist's ability allowed him to seek further legislative support from Rep. William Williamson.

Williamson introduced a bill requesting permission from the state of South Dakota to carve statues in Harney National Forest and on March 3, 1925, the bill became law.

Although the idea now had legal permission, money was still desperately needed before the project could begin. Borglum's enthusiasm led him to assure both Robinson and Norbeck that he could find contributors for the project. Early on he was very confident that public financial support would be forthcoming, but that was not always the case.

Originally Jefferson was on Washington's right, but was removed in 1934. PHOTO: JOE W. McCULLY

Borglum was going full speed ahead on Mount Rushmore, even though only few funds had been collected and no contract was in place. October 1, of 1925, Mount Rushmore held its first official dedication.

Dedication day was a great success. Crowds of people arrived, despite the bad roads, to witness the dedication day celebration. Sioux Indians in full regalia performed war dances, a band played and speeches were given by dignitaries, Gutzon Borglum and Senator Norbeck included. Huge flags of Spain, France, Great Britain and the colonial United States were raised and lowered, representing the former ownership of the territory, until finally a giant American flag was raised over the mountain while a band played *The Star Spangled Banner.*

The dedication was a great success and the South Dakotans seemed assured, for the first time, that a mountain carving would bring glory to their state. It seemed that there was nothing in the way– except the lack of money.

During August of 1926, Borglum returned to Keystone to take measurements of the mountain, paint carving marks and to bring models showing the design of the carving. His first plans called for the carving of three presidents, Washington, Lincoln and Jefferson. It was not until later that he, with the approval of Senator Norbeck, decided to add Theodore Roosevelt. The inclusion of a modern president generated a great deal of controversy.

It was easy for Gutzon Borglum to explain his decision regarding Washington, who was the father of our country and the first president; Thomas Jefferson, who authored the

Declaration of Independence, and the president who was responsible for the Louisiana Purchase which more than doubled the size of the United States. Abraham Lincoln was responsible for holding the country together during its greatest trial, the Civil War, and ending slavery in America.

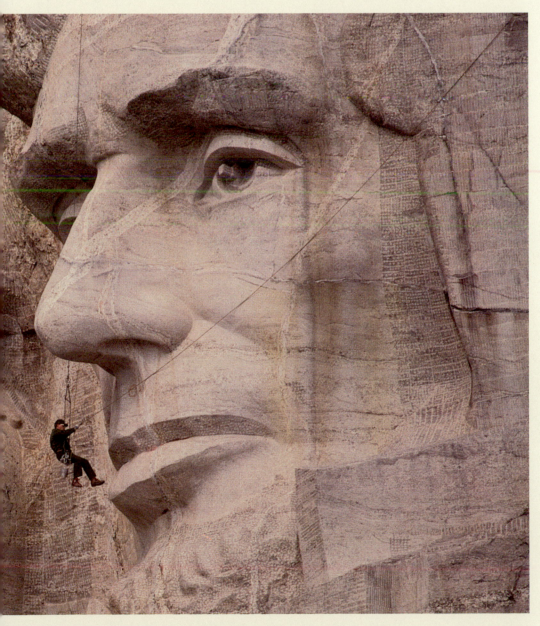

Otto "Red" Anderson chips stone away after the rock face was honeycombed. PHOTO: BELL STUDIOS

When it came to including President Theodore Roosevelt, Borglum was quite adamant. He felt that the 26th president should be honored for being a president who positioned himself on the side of the working man. Roosevelt had also worked hard to ensure the building of the Panama Canal, which Borglum believed to be part of the country's western expansion.

Although Borglum and his assistant, Major Tucker, had painted marks on the mountain in preparation of carving, work could not proceed until enough money was collected to purchase necessary equipment and pay would-be workmen. The project seemed to languish.

Luck arrived in the guise of President Calvin Coolidge, who decided to spend part of the summer of 1927 in the Black Hills. The state of South Dakota had done its best to entice the president with images of the prefect summer vacation spot. Their efforts paid off, and resulted in a big break for the Mount Rushmore memorial project.

Robinson, Senator Norbeck and the Mount Harney Association were unsuccessful in their earlier fund raising attempts but when news of a possible presidential visit got out, a few of the local business men, who knew their businesses would profit from the attention, finally decided to contribute to the Mount Rushmore memorial project.

The president and the first lady, Mrs. Grace Coolidge, stayed at the Game Lodge in Custer State Park and enjoyed South Dakota so much they decided to extend their visit from three weeks to three months.

President Coolidge, known as "Silent Cal" to the media for his lack of speech giving and hyperbole, had stated he would not make formal appearances while on vacation in South Dakota, but as he got to know more South Dakotans, he began to like them. To help out the state, and his new friends, he agreed to dedicate Mount Rushmore. To illustrate just what a man of few words President Coolidge was, a story was told of a Washington matron at a White House dinner party who approached the president and explained that she had made a wager with friends that she could get the president to say more than a couple of words. His reply was; "You lose."

To get Silent Cal to endorse Mount Rushmore was a major coup, but he did agree to a second

George Washington, Thomas Jefferson and Theodore Roosevelt faces under construction amidst a swarm of activity.
PHOTO BY CHARLES D'EMERY

dedication to celebrate the beginning of work on the memorial. It mattered little that there was not a real reason for the dedication, the promise of presidential support was reason enough for a gala celebration.

On August 10, 1927, President Coolidge put on his brand new cowboy hat, cowboy boots and chaps and mounted a steady horse for the trip up the mountain for the dedication.

After his speech, President Coolidge presented

Borglum with a set of drills. When Borglum stepped forward to accept the symbolic gift he announced, "As the first president who has taken part, please write the inscription to go on that mountain. We want your connection known in some other way than by your presence. I want the name of Calvin Coolidge on that mountain." What began as Borglum's impromptu invitation and gesture of good will, would later bring nothing but trouble.

Borglum took the drills and climbed to the top of the mountain, during which time a flag ceremony was performed. In amazement, the spectators watched as Borglum symbolically drilled the first holes into the mountain.

During the president's speech he told the crowd at Mount Rushmore that "their effort and courage entitles them to the sympathy and support of private beneficence and that of the national government." This was exactly the kind of endorsement the memorial needed.

The president was also kind enough to offer Gutzon Borglum the rights to his speech to copy and sell for fund raising piece and for promotional purposes.

It took a couple of months but finally, work on the memorial was underway and equipment was brought in. The carpenters began building stairs to the top

Washington profile viewed from the Borglum Memorial Highway (Hwy 244).
COURTESY NATIONAL PARK SERVICE

of the mountain, and a cable car was set up. And finally, the State of South Dakota began work on U.S. Highway 16, which had always been dreadful. Once the highway had been graveled, and a bridge built across the Missouri River, it was much easier for early tourists to get to the mountain.

Real drilling began on October 4, 1927, and the crew began testing tools and other equipment, logistics concerning exactly how they would carefully extract the rounded figures from the granite were gradually worked out.

The crew, which numbered at various times as many as 70 and as few as 4, was a sturdy group of men who had more experience working in the dark mines of the Black Hills than clinging to the sides of a mountain. Many had

Left: National Park Service worker Bob Crisman chips away at old sealer in a crack on the top of George Washington's head to remove the old material before refilling the crack with a new sealant material.
PHOTO BY PAUL HORSTED

already worked on Mount Rushmore installing stairs and buildings, and were glad to return, and became key employees who returned to work on the mountain at every chance. These men believed that they were working on an important piece of American history and came to love the project and admire the sculptor.

While Borglum could be very difficult to work with, or for, he was very good to his employees. "The Old Man," as they called him made sure they worked as safely as possible. His concern for them included special safety equipment and rules which were to be adhered to at all times. Because of his concern, very few injuries, and no deaths occurred during work on the mountain and most of his workers were as dedicated to him as to the carving.

Most of the men who worked on the mountain lived in the nearby town of Keystone. Days started early for these tough men, who were up well before dawn and at work by 7:00 a.m. in the summer, 7:30 a.m. in the fall and winter. Once they reached the mountain they had to climb the long stairway to the mountain top. Just getting to their jobs was a chore. Many of the men faced serious danger every day by either working with dynamite, detonator caps or hanging from cables on the face of the mountain. The workers faced harsh working conditions, the weather alone could break the strongest of men and the granite dust that crept into every crevice was almost impossible to wash away after the day was done.

Borglum with a bust of Abraham Lincoln.
PHOTO NATIONAL PARK SERVICE

These men played nearly as hard as they worked on the mountain. Borglum sponsored a baseball team that was quite successful. Weekends often found the men at honky-tonks where some spent time practicing their favorite pastimes... drinking and fighting.

In the fall of 1927, most of the work on the mountain consisted of blasting off the outer rock with dynamite to get to the unblemished granite below. Everyone, including Borglum, used this time to fine tune their working techniques and work on the mountain progressed until late November when the weather became unbearable and the money ran out.

Right: Talus slope at the base of Mount Rushmore. These large chunks of granite were removed from the mountain during carving, with some still showing signs of blast and drill marks.
PHOTO BY PAUL HORSTED

The concept of seeking government funding had been voiced by Norbeck, Borglum and Williamson in January of 1927. It was proving to be unrealistic to expect the private sector to fund the project. When the three men got together to discuss money, Norbeck suggested going to the Secretary of the Treasury, Andrew Mellon, to enlist his support in securing the necessary funds for the Mount Rushmore project. Norbeck would later come

The artist's model was changed nine times during the 14 years of Mount Rushmore's construction as the design changed or poor quality rock was encountered. It is shown here in its final form in Gutzon Boglum's second studio.   PHOTO: RISE STUDIO

to regret sending his friend Gutzon Borglum to Washington to ask for the secretary's help. Borglum asked Mellon for matching funds up to $250,000, which was only half of what he felt was needed to finish the project. Norbeck believed that Borglum could have received support for a full $500,000 from the secretary, and without any special terms.

Irritated at Borglum

but reconciled to make the best of the situation, Norbeck asked Congressman Williamson to draw up a bill authorizing the government to match private funding up to $250,000 but the bill received no support.

In 1928, the bill was reintroduced and, through the hard work of Senator Peter Norbeck, was passed in both the House and the Senate. It took until early 1929 for the House and Senate to fine tune the bill and on February 25, President Coolidge signed Public Law 805 of the 70th Congress. Terms of the law included "Not more than one-half the cost of such memorial and landscaping shall be borne by the United States, and not to exceed $250,000 is hereby authorized for the purpose...The appropriate proportionate share of the United States shall be advanced to said commission from time to time...to match the funds advanced from other sources."

The law also created a Mount Rushmore National Memorial Commission "to consist of twelve members who shall be appointed

Preceding Pages: An aspen, *Populus tremuloides,* in fall color forms a striking contrast to evergreen beauty of ponderosa pine, *Pinus ponderosa.*
PHOTO BY PAUL HORSTED

Detail of President Theodore Roosevelt's left eye, carved to create an illusion of a full pair of glasses. Borglum was a master in the art of implied and subtle nuances.   PHOTO BY PAUL HORSTED

by the President...a treasurer may be selected from outside the commission..." Coolidge, who had only days left in office, appointed John A. Boland, Fred W. Sargent, Lorine J. Spoonts, Charles Crane, Delos B. Gurney, Hale Holden, Joseph Cullinan, Frank O. Lowden, Charles M. Day and Julius Rosenwald. The two remaining positions were filled by newly elected Herbert Hoover who appointed South Dakota congressmen, William Williamson and Royal Johnson.

It was up to the new president to convene the new commission, and it took considerable maneuvering on Williamson's part to get the president to convene the meeting which would finally allow the Mount Rushmore National Memorial Commission to gain its official status. Primarily, those appointed to the commission were wealthy people who insiders felt would become involved and would then, hopefully, donate to the cause. This was not necessarily the case. Not appointed to the commission was the man who first dreamed of the monument, Doane Robinson. Senator Norbeck had been asked by President Hoover to accept an appointment, but knew how disappointed Robinson was and declined in a show of his solidarity. Both men were disappointed, but both still continued to support the Mount Rushmore memorial effort.

Finally, the government produced a check for $54,670.56, matching the full amount of money previously collected from private sources. The timing proved to be

Right: Park Service employees Karl Bachman and Bob Crisman inspect Thomas Jefferson's eye.
Below: January snow dusts Mount Rushmore.
PHOTOS BY PAUL HORSTED

fortuitous, for the year was 1929, and a stock market crash would throw America into a deep depression that would last for several years.

On the 4th of July, 1930, the Washington head was unveiled to an audience of around 2500. It was during this ceremony that the term "The Shrine of Democracy" was coined. The statement "America's Shrine for Political Democracy" was made by Chairman Cullinan, who presided over the ceremony.

During the ceremony an enormous flag covering the

Powderman John Johnson preparing dynamite charges.
PHOTO BY RISE STUDIO

Washington face was slowly raised to show an incomplete Washington gazing from the cliff. The ceremony greatly impressed onlookers who came to realize Borglum could do as he'd promised– deliver a mountain carving that could last for eons.

In the fall of 1931, work on the memorial stopped for a lack of funds. Even Borglum was broke and the commission's debts totalled over $16,000.

The crew was laid off and jobs were extremely scarce. Funds originally

designated "unemployment relief" were eventually distributed to the western end of South Dakota and Senator Norbeck was able to take $50,000, which was restricted to the hiring of the needy only, and get the government to match it with funds for the Mount Rushmore appropriation. His actions saved the project.

The new funds were used to pay off all debts, including the unpaid fees owed to Borglum, and finance

A steel drill bit being sharpened in the blacksmith shop. Mount Rushmore's hard granite dulled as many as 300 bits in a single day. PHOTO BELL STUDIO

The Mechanics of Carving on a Grand Scale...

Facing a project the size of a mountain had to be a daunting task for Gutzon Borglum. So how *does* one go about carving four 60 foot busts into a granite cliff? Borglum knew, and because he was able to overcome many difficulties to create a work with the nuances of smaller sculpture, he deserves the distinction of being considered one of the world's great sculptors.

When Borglum chose Mount Rushmore for his sculpture he faced a job requiring engineering skills in addition to artistic talent. Because of the deep cracks on the surface of the granite, Borglum knew he would have to remove the outer surface to find carvable granite, but he never knew just how far he would have to go to find the surface he needed. For Roosevelt's head he had to blast away as much as 100 feet before finding a suitable surface.

Borglum put into practice logistical systems he had developed at Stone Mountain. First, he had a network of stairs built so the workers could get to the top of the mountain. Once the stairs were in place an A-framed structure was built to bear the weight of the tramway cars which were used to haul supplies, and often Gutzon Borglum, to the top of the mountain.

One of the most important aspects of the job was an ability to translate the scale model's features to the face of Mount

A small portion of the more than 500 steps workers had to climb to reach the job every day.
PHOTO: RAPID CITY JOURNAL

Rushmore. Pointing was the technique used by Borglum to transfer measurements from the models to the mountain at a ratio of one inch to 1 foot.

Carving the 60 foot heads with the guidance of a 5 foot model was realized using a system adapted by the sculptor himself. After he chose the site for George Washington's head, Borglum implanted a metal pole vertically into what would be the center of the crown of Washington's head. He then placed a protractor, with its gauge in scale with one on the model, perpendicularly through the pole and used it for direction. The third element of the pointing system was a plumb line which dropped from a boom past the protractor where, by moving it back and forth and up and down, it could be used for location alignment and measurement.

Pointers marked the mountain to indicate where rock should be blasted. Drillers were then lowered down the cliff to drill holes which would be filled with small amounts of dynamite. This system worked so well that the workers could blast to within inches of the desired surface.

Borglum had workers form an egg shaped mass of rock so he could observe the play of light on the surface and decide how he wanted the face formed. He often changed the angle of the face, depending upon the type of rock uncovered and the effect of light upon the rock. Because of a vein of mineral laden rock, Borglum changed the position of the second Jefferson head so the vein ran across the cheek and lip instead of the nose.

Drillers were lowered over the cliff in metal and leather seats called bosun's chairs. Suspended by a cable controlled by a winch-man at the top of

Driller Jack Payne hangs from a bosun's chair to prepare the face of the mountain prior to carving President Lincoln's face.
PHOTO BELL STUDIOS

the mountain, the driller and winch-man could not see each other so a call-boy, attached to the top edge of the cliff by a leather belt, was posted between the two to relay instructions from one to the other.

Men working the side of the cliff had to adjust to unusual working conditions, including learning to walk both up and down the cliff at the same speed they were being raised or lowered by their winch-man. If they missed a step they could be dragged up or down the cliff like a limp rag doll.

Once enough rock had been blasted away remaining rock was refined by a technique that was called honeycombing. Workers using pneumatic drills bore holes a few inches apart to the required depth. A wedge and hammer were then used to knock off fairly large chunks of rock. Great care had to be taken to drill to the right depth because it was impossible to replace rock if too much was taken off. Finishing touches included "bumping," a process using pneumatic hammers with steel bits to smooth rock to the required texture.

The president's faces were smoothed to a texture similar to that of a concrete sidewalk, while a rougher texture was used to create the cravat, jacket and lapels on Washington, Roosevelt's mustache and Lincoln's beard.

Lincoln Borglum (right) and Jim LaRue, the chief pointer, operate the mast, boom and protractor of the pointing machine.
PHOTO RAPID CITY JOURNAL

A worker uses a drill as a "bumper" to smooth the inside of Lincoln's eye. Face high is the pupil.
PHOTO BY BELL STUDIO

another season of work on the mountain. From this point on, funding became easier to obtain, but altercations between the sculptor and the commission became harder to avoid.

In 1934, the Jefferson head, which had been started on Washington's right, was blasted away and a new position was found on Washington's left. The rock surrounding Washington's head was also blasted away at this time, allowing the

Interior of the winch house. A "call boy" relayed instructions from men in bosun chairs to winch operators. BELL STUDIO

face to stand out as never before.

During the Depression Norbeck, Williamson and Boland all had financial difficulties as South Dakota struggled additionally from drought and grasshopper infestation.

Borglum's discontent became more difficult for the members of the commission, particularly John A. Boland who was in charge of Mount Rushmore's finances. It took the intervention of Norbeck, who took Borglum to task for being so difficult, to smooth

tensions. It also took a loan from Boland to help Borglum keep his ranch, and to settle the artist down.

In 1934, tourism finally arrived in the Black Hills. Despite the depression, those who could afford to travel, did. Mount Rushmore was one of the places people visited in record numbers.

1934 also saw the revival of the Entablature, Borglum's vision of a brief history of America carved into the mountain near the faces. The Entablature had been the cause of trouble in 1930 when Borglum asked President Coolidge to write the history. Coolidge did and received plenty of publicity, not always flattering, from the press. It was discovered that Borglum, without Coolidge's consent, altered his work before presenting it to the press. The former president was furious. As far as Borglum was concerned, that was in the past and besides, Coolidge had died in 1933, leaving new opportunity for the Entablature. Borglum convinced the Hearst

newspaper chain to hold a competition for a best 600 word essay on American history and he convinced the Underwood Typewriter Co. to donate 22 typewriters as prizes and to contribute to advertising the contest.

Gutzon Borglum also convinced President

Workmen in bosun's chairs use pneumatic (air powered) drills to shape the face of President Abraham Lincoln in 1936.
PHOTO BY CHARLES D'EMERY

Franklin D. Roosevelt to be chairman of the judging committee. The grand prize winner would have his, or her, entry carved into the mountain beside the faces.

The publicity proved helpful to the Mount Rushmore project. Through the national newspaper coverage Borglum was able to find new presidential support for the memorial. From this encouragement Norbeck introduced a bill in the Senate authorizing additional funds and ending the matching requirement. His efforts were successful and funding was obtained.

1934 also saw the beginning of the end of the Boland-Borglum relationship. Borglum was again in dire financial straits and, as was his habit, he struck out at those around him. John

Right: Karl Bachman, a National Park Service employee, climbs down Abraham Lincoln's face during an inspection of Mount Rushmore.
PHOTO BY PAUL HORSTED

Boland was an easy choice since it was his job to control the project's costs. When the artist placed orders for goods or services without the proper authorization, John Boland would cancel them. This interference inflamed Gutzon Borglum, who began a four year long campaign to oust Boland. Ironically, Boland had personally bailed Borglum out of several financial problems. More than anyone else, Boland had supported the artist, but Borglum had a short term memory at best.

Blasting and drilling continued on the right of Jefferson's face for an appropriate place for President Theodore Roosevelt. Around 120 feet of surface rock had to be blasted away to find carvable granite. The Abraham Lincoln head was placed in the spot where the Entablature– which after all of the trials and tribulations with President Coolidge, and the national writing contest was

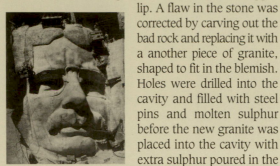

Theodore Roosevelt
PHOTO: BELL STUDIO

finally abandoned– was to have been.

The Jefferson face was refined, although the carvers had a problem with Jefferson's upper lip. A flaw in the stone was corrected by carving out the bad rock and replacing it with a another piece of granite, shaped to fit in the blemish. Holes were drilled into the cavity and filled with steel pins and molten sulphur before the new granite was placed into the cavity with extra sulphur poured in the cracks around the rock. This is the only patch that was needed on the entire Mount Rushmore memorial, and it was so well completed almost no one knows of its existence.

On August 30, 1936, an unveiling ceremony was held celebrating the near completion of the Jefferson face. Borglum, as always, created a ceremony to remember. President Franklin Roosevelt was in attendance, and although he had formerly declined to speak, when Borglum announced, "I want you, Mr. President, to dedicate this memorial as a shrine to democracy; to call upon the people of this earth for one hundred thousand years to come, to read the thought and to see what manner of men struggled here to establish self-determining government in the western world.

"I would ask this vast audience here, the people everywhere, to join in such a prayer," President Roosevelt replied.

"...I had seen the photograph, I had seen the drawings, and I had talked with those who are responsible for this great work, and yet I had no conception, until

Abraham Lincoln
PHOTO: BELL STUDIO

about ten minutes ago, not only of its magnitude, but also of its permanent beauty and importance.

...I think that we can perhaps meditate on those Americans of ten thousand years from now... Let us hope...they will believe we have honestly striven every day and generation to preserve a decent land to live in and a decent form of government to operate under."

In 1937, a bill promoting carving of a fifth figure on Rushmore was brought to Borglum's, and the committee's, attention. The proposed fifth figure would be Susan B. Anthony. This idea was promoted by the Equal Rights for Women organization as well as by Eleanor Roosevelt. Although Borglum and the committee opposed the idea, they were hesitant to make a fuss. They did not want to offend the First Lady or her husband. The matter was settled by Congress who attached a stipulation to Mount Rushmore funds that money could only be used on carvings in progress.

1937 was a banner year for work on Mount Rushmore. So much was accomplished that Borglum organized another dedication, this time for the Lincoln head. The dedication was set for September 17, 1937, which was also the 150th anniversary of the Constitution.

Unlike past dedications, no luminaries were present and Borglum decided to commemorate the men who had influenced the project but

Left: Tim Vogt, assisted by Dennis Laughlin at the top of Thomas Jefferson's head, climbs down Jefferson's face in a geologic study of the cracks in the Mount Rushmore memorial.
PHOTO BY PAUL HORSTED

were now deceased.

When Borglum stepped to the platform to speak he said; "I will now call the roll of those whose understanding, sympathy, and instant aid has made this great memorial possible: Calvin Coolidge, Andrew Mellon, Coleman Dupont, Edward Rushmore, Julius Rosenwald, J. S. Cullinan, Bruce Yates, Dr. O'-Hara, Peter Norbeck. They are with the gods! We will keep their faith! We will carry on!"

Thomas Jefferson
PHOTO: BELL STUDIO

Then, from the top of the Washington head, a lone bugler played Taps. It was an emotion charged moment for everyone present.

1938 was an important year for Borglum. He was finally able to oust the committee who had so irritated him for years. With the help of his old friends, United States Congressman Kent Keller of Illinois and Senator Key Pittman

of Nevada, Gutzon Borglum was given almost complete control over the memorial. He was able to hand-pick his own commission and was accountable only to Congress until July of 1939 when the National Park Service stepped in to control the project.

Work progressed at a rapid pace and on July 2, 1939, a dedication of the Roosevelt carving took place. 12,000 people attended, as well as a famous tenor who sang *God Bless America*, a new song by Irving Berlin. Finally, with fireworks blazing, a floodlight lit up the face of Roosevelt. The crowd was in awe.

March 6, 1941, John Gutzon de le Mothe Borglum died from complications from surgery. His son, Lincoln, who had been an employee of the project since 1934, had worked his way up in the ranks to full superintendent in 1938. When his father died Lincoln Borglum became head sculptor for the Mount Rushmore memorial.

Officially appointed by the Mount Rushmore National Memorial Commission, Lincoln finish-

ed the carving "in accordance with the known plans, models, and specifications of the late

Nearly four hundred men spent more than fourteen years working on the Mount Rushmore National Memorial.
PHOTO COURTESY NATIONAL PARK SERVICE

Gutzon Borglum."

Because it was the eve of the United States' involvement in World War II, Lincoln realized he should complete as much as possible before funding ran out for good. He finished the faces as much as was possible and left many areas of the project planned by his father unfinished.

Gutzon had planned on finishing each figure to the waist, completing the Hall of Records and a stone stairway. He wanted the mounds of broken rock removed below the carvings. None of these things were completed to either Gutzon, or Lincoln, Borglum's satisfaction.

Lincoln had the surface of the faces sealed with a composite consisting of equal parts of linseed oil, white lead and granite dust to retard weathering, and oversaw the removal of machinery and equipment from the memorial.

Lincoln promoted the completion of the Hall of Records, which would have an inscription of the history of the United States and biographies of the presidents

George Washington
PHOTO: BELL STUDIO

carved on the mountains carved into its walls.

After more than fifty years have passed since Lincoln ended the project and finally a modified version of the Hall of Records is scheduled to be completed by the end of 1997. It will have porcelain and enamel panels in the floor and be permanently sealed.

The project lasted 14 years with only 6½ years of actual carving time. The full cost of Mount Rushmore National Memorial totalled $989,992.32, with $836,000 paid with federal funds. Not a bad price for a memorial visited by more than two million people a year.

MISHAPS ON THE MOUNTAIN...

The physical logistics of carving a memorial the size of Mount Rushmore posed unique problems for the construction crew. Although many of the workmen were former miners who had worked under extreme conditions, none of them had any experience carving mountains.

These men faced unusual and dangerous working conditions every day. Some worked packing dynamite and others spent their days suspended in bosun's chairs swinging over the face of the mountain guiding pneumatic drills, suspended by chains attached to the drillers cable, into the side of the mountain.

Supported only by a cable, attached to a winch at the top of the mountain, the safety of the men depended upon safe equipment and the attention of the winch operators whose job was to reel them up and down as needed.

Borglum placed a high priority on the safety of his men, making sure they wore masks to prevent breathing granite dust and insisting they work in staggered layers so that if material, or equipment fell, those below would not get hurt.

Mount Rushmore's safety record is really quite remarkable considering the dangerous work that was involved. In 6½ years of dynamiting and drilling, few serious accidents occurred and, remarkably, there were no fatalities. Deaths were later associated with the project when two men died of silicosis, caused by inhaling granite dust.

A near-miss involved a runaway tram car with five men traveling to the mountain top. A screw on the brake came loose and the tram plummeted back down the cable towards the base. A foreman and a mechanic were able to slow the speeding car down and only one man was

Gutzon and Lincoln Borglum in a tram cage. On June 2, 1940, the tram cage broke loose near the top of the mountain and sent five men hurtling to the platform below.
PHOTO BY CHARLES D'EMERY

seriously hurt from injuries that occurred as he jumped from the car before it hit the platform.

Working in extreme weather conditions, it was no wonder one of the more serious accidents occurred when lighting struck the mountain and blew the shoes entirely off a worker. It also set dynamite caps to blasting and shocked several other workmen. From then on men took cover from storms in shacks on top of the mountain.

Regular near-misses were part of the work on the mountain. One day the massive A-frame structure that held the tramway cable was flung from the top of the mountain when a guy cable snapped. Workmen had just left the platform to return to work after lunch as the cable snapped and the A-frame went flying over the side. Just a few minutes earlier and several workers would have been flung over the side as well.

FLORA AND FAUNA...

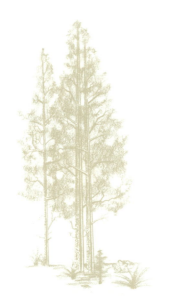

From afar, the dark color of the ponderosa pine, *Pinus ponderosa,* the most common tree in the Black Hills, led the Oglala Indians to name the area Paha Sapa, literally high black. These trees thrive in the dry soil of the Black Hills area because of their taproots which extend deep into soil to find moisture. Ponderosa pine was named by Scottish botanist David Douglas, in 1826, for its extremely heavy, or ponderous, wood.

The Black Hills have been described as an island of mountains floating in a sea of plains. As the only mountains in an otherwise flat South Dakota this seems as apt a description as any.

The Black Hills are considered an eastern extension of the Rocky Mountains. The Oglala Indians called the area Paha Sapa, Sapa meaning black and Paha indicating height. The Hills rise to 7242 feet at Harney Peak, the highest point east of the Rocky Mountains, with the average elevation between 3000 and 4300 feet. Although an elevation of 7200 feet definitely qualifies the area as mountainous, the name Black Hills has persisted.

As an island of mountains, the Black Hills support an interesting assortment of plant life. Positioned very close to the center of the continent, the Hills consist of several ecotones, or places where plant communities meet and mingle. Four separate vegetative systems play a significant role in the Black Hills; the Rocky Mountain coniferous forest system, made up of mostly ponderosa pine; the northern coniferous forest system; a Great Plains grassland system; and a deciduous forest system which also includes a heavy shrub influence.

The ponderosa pine, *Pinus ponderosa*, is the most dominant tree in the Black Hills, and the major component in the Rocky Mountain coniferous forest system and the most common pine in North America. These tolerant trees thrive in dry climates where their taproots can plunge deep into the earth in search of water. Ponderosa pine most often grow above the 4000 foot level.

Creeping cedar, *Juniperus horizontalis*, as well as quaking aspen, *Populus tremuloides*, are also found in and around the ponderosa pine forests. Aspen can more often be found on the edges of the pine forests.

The lodgepole pine, *Pinus contorta*, which is much more commonly found in the Bighorn and Laramie Mountain Ranges of Wyoming, over 150 miles away, inhabits about 150 acres in the Nahant Area of the Hills. Limber pine, *Pinus flexilis,* can be found in the Cathedral Spires area of the Hills and around the summit of Little Devil's Tower. Limber pine, as its name implies, can withstand strong wind and heavy snows by bending, instead of breaking. The average age of the trees in the Limber Pine Natural Area is 123 years. Limber Pine grow in elevations of 6600 to 6800 feet.

Growing in the northern areas of the Black Hills is the white spruce, *Picea glauca*, which is identified with the Northern Coniferous forest system. Normally found much farther to the north, white spruce can usually be found on north facing slopes in fairly dense groves in places where water is more accessible. Old man's beard, *Alectoria sarmentosa*, commonly found hanging in the lower branches of spruce and the understory includes moss, fern, lichen,

Left: The carved faces of the presidents witness the changing colors of autumn on paper birch trees, *Betula papyrifera,* among the evergreen ponderosa pine standing nearby.
PHOTO BY JEFF GNASS

Right: An alert mule deer, *Odocoileus hemionus,* looks up from grazing. Named because of their large ears, these graceful animals can be found all over South Dakota.
PHOTO BY JEFF GNASS

and several exotic flowers including bracted orchid, *Habenaria viridis*, Yellow lady's slipper, *Cypripedium calceolus,* and Venus' slipper, *Viburnum lentago* which grow in abundance.

In lush cool canyons where streams meander both above and below ground, the deciduous system includes ferns, sedges and meadow rue, crowfoot, thistle, bulrushes, wild geraniums, horsetail, dogbane and plenty of poison ivy.

In the northern end of the Hills, lush deciduous forests include bur oak, *Quercus macrocarpa*, box elder, *Acer negundo*, cottonwood, *Populus deltoides*, as well as peach leaf willow, *Salix amygdaloides*, which is often found thriving by stream banks. The most common willow found in the Black Hills is Bebb's willow, *Salix bebbiana*, although several factors including insect damage and over-clearing for grazing have affected its growth and reduced its numbers. Bebb's and peach leaf willows are still abundant, growing to heights of more than 12 feet.

At one time a distinct shrub zone indicated the places where forest gradually changed to grassland, but the declining level of the underground water table has seriously affected its

Above: Blue skies over a rolling meadow filled with the pink blooms of wild bergamot, *Monarda fistulosa*, in the Black Hills of South Dakota.
PHOTO BY DENNIS FLAHERTY

Calypso bulbosa. Grasses also thrive in these areas, as do shrubs such as the serviceberry, *Amelanchier alnifolia*, and the nannyberry,

Pasque flower, a member of the buttercup family, is the state flower of South Dakota
PHOTO BY PAUL HORSTED

growth, although healthier shrub zones can still be found in some areas. Where these zones

are still healthy kinnikinnick, *Arctostaphylos uva-ursi,* and snowberry, *Albus occidentalis,* can be found near open meadows and floodplains in the central Hills. In some areas cinquefoil, *Potentilla fruticosa,* appears in areas between the forest and grasslands.

Sagebrush grows in the lowlands of the Hills and the most proliferate is the common sagebrush, *Artemisia tridentata,* which grows well in dry soil. Sandsage, *Artemisia filifolia,* grows in sandier areas.

Other vegetation found in lower, drier areas of the Black Hills include mountain mahogany, *Cercocarpus montanus,* which, when found in higher locations, can grow to over 10 feet high. Often found growing near the mountain

Above: Chinese ring-necked pheasant, the state bird of South Dakota, was introduced to the area in 1898 and is known for its colorful plumage.
PHOTO BY LEN RUE, JR.

mahogany is the western redcedar, *Juniperus scopulorum* and sumac, *Rhus trilobata.*

In the grassland areas which surround the Hills the predominant grasses are green needlegrass, *Stipa viridula,* buffalo grass, *Buchloe dactyloides,* western wheatgrass, *Agropyron smithii,* side-oats grama, *Bouteloua curtipendula,* little bluestem, *Andropogon scoparius,* prairie junegrass, *Koeleria pyramidata,* blue grama, *Bouteloua gracilis,* and prairie cordgrass, *Spartina pectinata* are found. Japanese chess, *Bromus japonicus,* and cheat grass, *Bromus dactyloides,* are species that were

Right: Bighorn sheep rams in a meadow. These majestic animals feed on ground cover.
PHOTO BY PAUL HORSTED

Left: Mountain goats poised on granite boulders in the Black Hills of South Dakota.
PHOTO BY PAUL HORSTED

introduced to the area many years ago.

Other plants found in the grasslands are the forbs prairie clovers, *Petalostemum,* leadplant, *Amorpha canascens,* prickly pear, *Opuntia,* partridge pea, *Cassia fasciculata,* and the yucca, *Yucca glauca,* as well as dozens of other species. It should be noted that the condition of the grasslands that surround the Black Hills is determined by usage. If over grazed, only the shorter sedges and grasses will be present. Also, ponderosa pine seems to invade grassland areas but the occurrence of forest fires keeps the encroachment in check.

Flowers appear in both dry and moist areas of the Black Hills. Blue larkspur, *Delphinium nuttalianum,* Rocky Mountain iris, *Iris missouriensis,* fleabane, *Erigeron,* asters, *Aster,* yarrow, *Achillea millefolium,* wild bergamot, *Monarda fistulosa,* sego lily, *Calochortus nuttallii,* sunflowers, *Helianthus,* and black-eyed Susan, *Rudbeckia hirta,* wood lily, *Lililum philadelphicum,* Indian paintbrush, *Castilleja sessiliflora,* and goldenrod, *Solidago,* bloom at different times throughout the year.

Above: An alert coyote, *Canis latrans,* pauses in the snow to listen for the sounds of danger. These adaptable animals can survive in many environments and feed on rodents and other small animals.
PHOTO BY LEN RUE, JR.

The Hills play host to more than 60 species of mammals, and over 130 bird species appear in the Black Hills during all or part of the year. Most of the mammals are considered widespread and can be found throughout the Hills, but a few can only be found in certain areas. The Rocky Mountain goats, *Oreamnos americanus,* are generally found only in the granite peaks of the Harney Range. These heavily coated animals are not native to the area, but were brought to Custer State Park, just south

FLORA AND FAUNA CONTINUED...

of Mount Rushmore, in 1924, as a gift from Canada. From the original gift of 6 goats, there are now over 200 roaming freely throughout the Mount Rushmore area.

The American Bison, *Bison bison*, is the largest mammal in the Black Hills area. Once the most plentiful animal in North America, the bison was hunted to near extinction in the late 1800s. These large animals can weigh as much as 2000 pounds and are often found roaming in large herds throughout Custer State Park and at Wind Cave National Park.

Other mammals found in the Hills include pronghorn, *Antilocapra americana*, which are often called antelope. These swift animals can maintain long distance speeds of up to 50 miles per hour.

Blacktail prairie dog, *Cynomys ludovicianus*, are native of the area. This small rodent gets its name from the bark it makes when it warns other prairie dogs of impending danger. Least chipmunks, *Eutamias minimus*,

Above: A meadow rose and grasshopper. Grasshoppers were responsible for wiping out crops in the state in the mid-1870s.
PHOTO BY PAUL HORSTED

are natives that can be found in almost every area of the Hills.

Red Squirrel, *Tamiasciurus hudsonicus*, bighorn sheep, *Ovis canadensis*, another species introduced to the area, bobcat, *Lynx rufus*, elk or wapiti, *Cervus canadensis*, and the coyote, *Canis latrans*, which is the state animal, are all found in the area. The white tail deer, *Odocoileus virginianus*, and mule deer, *Odocoileus hemionus*, are also seen in the Black Hills. Other animals include the beaver, *Castor canadensis*, which were once quite abundant but their numbers have been so reduced that new stock had to be introduced to the area. The porcupine, *Erethizon dorsatum*, is common in the Black Hills, as is the yellow-bellied marmot, *Marmota flaviventris*, a native species that can be found in many areas of the Black Hills.

The mountain lion, *Felis concolor*, is only

occasionally seen, and the black bear, *Ursus americanus*, is no longer in the area. The gray wolf, *Canis lupus*, was once common to the Black Hills but is now considered extinct.

Birds are abundant in the Black Hills and

Above: Bull elk with doe and calf. Once hunted to extinction, elk, also called wapiti, were reintroduced to the Black Hills and now have a large population in the area. A mature bull elk can weigh as much as 1100 pounds.
PHOTO BY LEN RUE, JR.

because of the Hills' central North American location, many western and eastern species come together in this area. Lewis' woodpecker, northern three-toed woodpecker, pinon jay, gray jay, solidary vireo, white-winged junco, poor-will, Cassin's finch, mountain bluebird, Audubon's warbler and the dipper can all be seen flitting around areas of the Black Hills. Turkey vulture, golden eagle, red-tailed hawk, northern flicker, ruffed grouse, rock wren, ovenbird and the western tanger can also be seen in the Black Hills area.

Because of the drier, colder climate of the area there are relatively few amphibians and reptiles that live here. A few species of frogs, turtles, lizards and snakes do make their home in the Black Hills.

The ponderosa pine and white spruce forests of the Black Hills, along with the prairie grassland and shrubbery combine to create natural habitats for the many creatures that come from east, west, north and south to co-mingle in this island of mountains in the sea of grass.

Left: This bison herd is just a small portion of more than 1400 head that roam the Black Hills.
PHOTO BY PAUL HORSTED

Right: Pronghorn, *Antilocapra americana,* buck. Often called antelope, these swift animals can easily reach speeds of up to 60 miles per hour.
PHOTO BY LEONARD LEE RUE III

UNFINISHED DREAMS...

The Entablature, as envisioned by Gutzon Borglum in this enhanced photo, was to be an inscription of a brief history of the United States. The proposed Entablature was to have been 80 by 120 feet and in the shape of the Louisiana Purchase. The plan was abandoned when it was realized that in order to read the inscription from a distance, each letter would have to be so large that there would be no room for all the words.
PHOTO COURTESY NATIONAL PARK SERVICE

When Gutzon Borglum first envisioned a mountain monument he believed a carving honoring the four American presidents would be incomplete without a written explanation of the accomplishments of the country they represented. Borglum's opinion was, "You may as well drop a letter into the world's postal service without an address or signature as to send that carved mountain into history without identification."

As some of Borglum's first notes and sketches indicate, he envisioned an inscription of 80 by 120 feet carved into the east wall of the mountain. In 1926, he decided that the west wall, behind the heads, would be the better location for the entablature until, after another change of mind, he decided to place it in the current location of the Lincoln head.

In 1927, President Calvin Coolidge gave the dedication speech officially beginning the work on Mount Rushmore. At the end of the speech Coolidge gave Borglum a set of drills. When Borglum stepped forward to accept the symbolic gift he announced, "As the first president who has taken part, please write the inscription to go on that mountain. We want your connection known in some other way than by your presence. I want the name of Coolidge on that mountain." Borglum's impromptu announcement brought much needed publicity to Mount Rushmore and cemented President Coolidge's support for the memorial.

Borglum decided that the inscription should commemorate nine major events in American history; the Declaration of Independence; the framing of the Constitution; the Louisiana Purchase; the admission of Texas to the Union; the ceding of the Floridas to the United States; the Oregon boundary settlement; the acquisition of California; the Alaska purchase and the cutting of the Panama Canal. The central theme of these historical events is the expansion of America through Manifest Destiny, the belief that America had a right and duty to expand across North America.

When Coolidge, who had agreed to follow the outline created by Borglum, submitted his manuscript of the first two topics, a flood of newspaper coverage followed. Unfortunately, the newspapers were not all that kind with regards to Coolidge's text. Soon after, it was discovered that Borglum had revised Coolidge's work without the former president's knowledge or his consent.

The original Coolidge version read: The Declaration of Independence–The eternal right to seek happiness through self-government and the divine duty to defend that right at any sacrifice." Borglum's version was: "In the year of our Lord 1776 the people declared the eternal right to seek happiness, self-government and the divine duty to defend that right at any sacrifice."

President Coolidge's second chapter read:

Left: This aerial view of Mount Rushmore shows the entrance to the Hall of Records in the canyon behind the heads. The Hall of Records was to have been a vault-like museum housing many of America's most important records. Borglum believed that there should be some explanation of the culture of the presidents carved on the mountain, and inscriptions detailing specific events in American history carved into the walls of the Hall of Records.
PHOTO BY RUSS FINLEY

Right: After 50 years, an interior wall in the incomplete Hall of Records still shows marks indicating where and how deep the next drilling holes were to be placed.
PHOTO BY PAUL HORSTED

"The constitution-charter of perpetual union of free people of sovereign states establishing a government of limited powers–under an independent president, congress, and court, charged to provide security for all citizens in their enjoyment of liberty, equality and justice under the law." The Borglum revision read: "In 1787 assembled in convention they made a charter of perpetual union for free people of sovereign states establishing a government of limited powers under an independent president, congress, and court charged to provide security for all citizens in their enjoyment of liberty, equality and justice."

The Hall of Records, located in a small canyon behind the Mount Rushmore carvings. New construction on the Hall is scheduled to be completed late 1997.   PHOTO BY PAUL HORSTED

Although many felt Borglum's changes were an improvement on Coolidge's work, the press lambasted him for editing the former president's text. One headline read: "Borglum Shows Coolidge How." Argument arose as to whether or not Borglum had a right to revise Coolidge's writings. Members of the Mount Rushmore Memorial Commission believed that Borglum was, by law, ultimately responsible for what appeared on the mountain, so the final decision regarding Coolidge's text was up to Borglum.

Coolidge, disgusted by the whole fiasco, never completed his manuscript and severed ties with Borglum. The only good to come of the episode was the huge amount of publicity generated for the Mount Rushmore project.

The Entablature was revived in 1934 when the Hearst newspapers ran a contest inviting citizens to submit a 600 word essay memorializing the history of America using the nine episodes Borglum previously had outlined.

Borglum invited then President Franklin Delano Roosevelt to be chairman of the national committee of judges which included several Senators, university presidents and many other notables including Mrs. Roosevelt.

The tone of the contest implied the winner would have their entry carved on the face of Mount Rushmore, but in reality, that wouldn't happen. Public Law 805 of the 70th Congress determined "a suitable inscription to be indited by Calvin Coolidge." By law Coolidge was the only person who could write the inscription.

While the contest received more than 800,000 entries, the carving of the Entablature was never to be. Borglum realized the letters would have to be so large that there would not be enough room for all the words. Also, relocation of the Jefferson head forced a relocation of the Lincoln head to the area originally planned for the inscription.

Nebraskan William Burkett won the college edition grand prize, a college scholarship. Today, a bronze plaque bearing Burkett's essay is located at the Borglum View Terrace.

Above: Wall inside the Hall of Records shows drill marks left behind more than 50 years ago. Below: The interior of the Hall of Records.
PHOTOS BY PAUL HORSTED

Another idea never completed was the Hall of Records. In 1936, Borglum wrote to Senator Peter Norbeck of his intentions to carve out an area in the canyon behind the heads for a great hall. This hall, or museum, would have

an area of 80 by 100 feet. Bronze and glass cabinets would hold important historical documents engraved on aluminum, rolled and placed in protective tubing.

He later changed his plans to include the addition of several rooms which would hold proof of the advances of civilization. Electricity, medicine, art, communications and air travel were examples of the types of advances that would be represented in the archives. He would also include a section explaining the creation of Mount Rushmore, along with a bronze and gold plated bas-relief showing the history of the "West World."

Borglum envisioned a grand staircase carved out of granite leading up to a 22 1/2 foot wide entrance with glass doors leading to a 44 foot tall panel which would be topped by a 38 foot wide flying eagle. On the panel the words: "America's Onward March," and "The Hall of Records" would be inscribed. The great hall would be filled with statues of Benjamin Franklin, John Hancock and other noteworthy Americans. About the great Hall, Borglum said "If such an exhibition could be provided, the world a thousand years from now would have something interesting and educational to look at." He probably would have been proven right.

Borglum had his workers blast a 70 foot tunnel into the mountain between July 1938 and July 1939. To the consternation of both Gutzon and Lincoln Borglum, the Hall was never completed. Both men fervently believed that not leaving a permanent record of the history of America and the civilized world was doing a disservice to peoples of the future who may wonder what the colossal mountain carving stood for, just as we wonder today about the significance of Stonehenge and the mystery of the cultures responsible for leaving behind the giant carved heads on Easter Island or the great stone cities of the Southwest.

THE SON ALSO SHINES...

Lincoln Borglum was only twelve years old when he arrived, with his father Gutzon Borglum, in the Black Hills for the first time on September 24, 1924.

Born April 9, 1912, James Lincoln Borglum was used to accompanying his famous father whenever he traveled. Gutzon believed that real life experiences were the best way for a boy to learn about life so he took his son when he was working on commissions and on his speaking engagements. Gutzon even used his newborn son's

Lincoln Borglum in 1939.
PHOTO: BELL STUDIO

likeness on baby faces he added to a fountain he was working on for Bridgeport, Connecticut.

On their first trip to the hills, father and son hiked and rode horseback through the granite outcroppings of the Harney Range. They viewed the rugged peaks of the Needles, but the famous sculptor felt the peaks were not ideal for carving. Lincoln and his father left South Dakota without discovering the right place for an undertaking of such magnitude.

Almost a year later, in August 1925, father and son returned to the South Dakota hills to scout a location for the proposed mountain carving. Guides brought them to the perfect

Mount Rushmore in 1925.
PHOTO: RISE STUDIO

location, a massive granite mountain whose face had a southeast exposure, Mt. Rushmore.

While he was in High School, he assisted his father by driving the first model of the carving to the Black Hills from San Antonio, Texas. Unfortunately, Lincoln fell asleep while driving and when the car rolled, the base of the model broke. Luckily, no one was hurt and necessary repairs were made to both the car

and the model of Mount Rushmore.

Lincoln spent many summers working with his father on Mount Rushmore and in 1932 when the pointer, the person who directed measuring, was fired by Gutzon, Lincoln was asked to help out on a temporary basis. Lincoln had planned on attending the University of Virginia later that fall, but he wanted to help his father, so he stayed on as pointer.

It wasn't until 1934 that Lincoln began to get paid for his services and his first official job earned him a whopping 55 cents per hour.

Lincoln's career on Mount Rushmore progressed from pointer to working with explosives, to jackhammering, to foreman, to full superintendent in 1938. When his father died unexpectedly in 1941, Lincoln Borglum became the project's sculptor.

Officially appointed by the Mount Rushmore National Memorial Commission, Lincoln would go on to finish the carving "in accordance with the known plans, models, and specifications of the late Gutzon Borglum." It was the eve of the United States' involvement in World War II and Lincoln realized that he should finish as much as he could before funding ran out for good. He finished the faces as much as was possible and left many areas of the project his father had planned unfinished. Gutzon had planned on finishing each figure to the waist, completing the Hall of Records and its stone stairway, and removing the mounds of broken rock from below the carvings. None of these things were ever completed to either Gutzon or Lincoln Borglum's satisfaction.

Lincoln had the surface of the faces sealed with a composite consisting of equal parts of linseed oil, white lead and granite dust to retard weathering, and he oversaw the removal of the machinery and heavy equipment

Right: In 1941, Lincoln Borglum ended carving on Mount Rushmore National Memorial, a project undertaken by his father, Gutzon Borglum, in 1927.
PHOTO BY DICK DIETRICH

from the mountain top of the memorial.

Lincoln continued to urge the completion of the Hall of Records, a room cut into a small canyon behind the carved faces, which would have an inscription of the history of the United States carved into its walls as well as an explanation

Lincoln Boglum brought the Mount Rushmore National Memorial project to a close in 1941.
PHOTO COURTESY NATIONAL PARK SERVICE

of the people who were carved on the mountain. His urging fell on deaf ears. Funds were finally cut off due to the onset of World War II. After more than 50 years, the Hall of Records is finally scheduled for completion by the end of 1997.

In October of 1941, the same month carving was brought to an end, Lincoln was appointed the first National Park Service Superintendent at Mount Rushmore, a position he filled until 1943.

PRESIDENTS FOR POSTERITY...

Washington en route to Fort Le Boeuf to deliver an ultimatum to the French. THE BETTMAN ARCHIVE

"Precedents are dangerous things; let the reins of government then be braced and held with a steady hand, and every violation of the Constitution be reprehended: if defective let it be amended, but not suffered to be trampled upon whilst it has an existence."

George Washington
1786

George Washington, the first president of the United States of America, was born in Westmoreland County, Virginia, on February 11, 1732. The son of Augustine and Mary Ball Washington, George had two older half brothers, Lawrence and Augustine, three brothers; Samuel, Charles, and John Augustine and one sister, named Betty.

His father was a land owner and businessman who died when George was only 11 years old. His mother would not allow George the benefit of an English education, so he was educated in Virginia. He often sought guidance from his half-brother Lawrence, who was 14 years older. After Lawrence died, George inherited his estate, Mount Vernon.

Washington was a surveyor as a young man.
THE BETTMAN ARCHIVE

In his teens, Washington grew to be over six-feet tall and weighed about 180 pounds. He was considered an attractive man and, although it is true he eventually wore dentures, contrary to popular belief, he never had wooden teeth pounded into his gums.

Even as a young man, his serious demeanor and innate integrity made him popular with his neighbors and friends. Very early on he developed personal standards he would live by for the rest of his life. Perhaps it was his reputation of a man of integrity that led to the fable concerning his cutting down a cherry tree and admitting his discretion to his father as he supposedly said: "I cannot tell a lie, I did it."

It is possible that because he had not been educated in England, he did not adopt superior airs common in his day, allowing him to earn the respect and affection of men from all the classes. At the same time, because he was born a Virginia aristocrat, he was very highly regarded by his peers.

A man of many sterling qualities, George Washington inspired loyalty because his own personal standards included modesty, a lack of pretension, consideration of others, honesty, humility, and an unassuming manner. Although known to have a temper, he usually displayed a contemplative demeanor that was often misconstrued as aloof. He was also well known for

Washington, at age 40, in uniform.
THE BETTMAN ARCHIVE

having one of the best minds of his era and was respected by most.

On June 21, 1731, George Washington married a 27 year old widow, Martha Dandridge Custis. Although the couple had no children together,

Left: The George Washington figure was the first carving started, and completed, on Mount Rushmore. Washington, the first president of the United States, was also commander in chief of the Continental Army.
PHOTO BY RUSS FINLEY

Right: Profile of George Washington. Sculptor Borglum gave the most prominent position on Mount Rushmore to President Washington.
PHOTO BY PAUL HORSTED

Martha's two children were always treated by Washington as his own and he took great pleasure in their company.

Before becoming involved in politics, he was a surveyor for Culpepper County, Virginia. In 1752, he became a major in the Virginia militia, the first of several military appointments. He proved to be a brave and inspiring leader. In 1755, while he was an aide-de-camp to General Edward Braddock during the French and Indian War, he had his horse shot out from under him on two occasions, yet he never wavered in his actions. When General Braddock was killed in the battle, Washington was able to rally the forces and his reputation as a leader grew.

Washington at Valley Forge in the winter of 1777–78.
VALLEY FORGE HISTORICAL SOCIETY

Although Washington was a Virginian, he agreed with Northerners who protested British taxation. Although at first he believed that a peaceful reconciliation with England should be negotiated, he soon realized the colonies must declare their independence. In 1775, at the urging of John Adams, he was appointed commander in chief of the Continental Army.

After two years of battles, some won and some lost, Washington and his army wintered at Valley Forge– without food, blankets and most men without shoes. Many died during the long winter of 1777–78, but in the spring news of support from France, who recognized the independence of America and provided aid to the Continental Army, justified the sacrifices.

Washington and his troops forced the surrender of the British at Yorktown. Soon after the treaty was signed, he resigned his commission as commander in chief and returned to his Mount Vernon plantation.

Washington directing the planting at Mount Vernon.
THE BETTMAN ARCHIVE

When the newly formed United States elected a president, it was only natural that George Washington would be the unanimous choice. He was elected to two terms and he served his country as president from April 30, 1789 until March 3, 1797.

As the first president, Washington set dozens of precedents for future American leaders, including many that remain in place today. He relied on the advice of his cabinet, which he personally chose, he served only two terms, a precedent that remained unbroken until 1940, when President Franklin Delano Roosevelt was elected to a 3rd and 4th term (during FDR's 4th term he signed into law a bill restricting future presidents to only two terms in office). When Washington

Washington resigning as commander in chief in 1783.
THE LIBRARY OF CONGRESS

was faced with appointing a chief justice of the Supreme Court, he went outside the bench for his selection, instead of appointing a senior member, disregarding the issue of seniority.

Washington signed bills creating the office of postmaster general, the first federal census, the U.S. Mint in Philadelphia, the Department of State, the Department of War and the Department of the Treasury. During his term, the Bill of Rights was ratified, setting forth the standards that made America one of the greatest democracies in the world.

George Washington retired to Mount Vernon in 1797, however, he was again commissioned lieutenant general and commander in chief of the American forces for a brief time because of a threat of war with France. He never again saw battle and returned to retirement. He died at home on December 14, 1799.

Thomas Jefferson, the third president of the United States, is best remembered as the author of the Declaration of Independence. He began his presidential career on March 4, 1801, when he walked through the streets of Washington, D.C. to the partially completed Capitol.

A tall man with red hair and hazel eyes, he was very slim with a long neck and chiseled features. He was very casual in dress, often to the disapproval of others.

Born April 13, 1743, on the Shadwell plantation in Virginia, to Colonel Peter Jefferson, a landowner and public servant, and Jane Randolph Jefferson, about whom little is known. He had one brother and six sisters; Randolph, Anna, Lucy, Martha, Elizabeth, Mary and Jane. His father moved the family to Tuckahoe in order to fulfill an obligation as executor of the will of his late friend, William Randolph, by residing at Tuckahoe plantation and caring for the man's orphaned children. The Jefferson family stayed at Tuckahoe for six years before returning to Shadwell.

Young Jefferson was a studious youth who became an outstanding

Thomas Jefferson
PORTRAIT BY GILBERT STUART

student. He was fluent in French, Latin and Greek and studied the classics in their initial languages. At seventeen, Jefferson enrolled at

the College of William and Mary where he studied literature, mathematics, science and philosophy. In 1762, he studied law under George Wythe and in 1767, became a lawyer.

He had several romances before meeting and marrying Martha Wayles Skelton on January 1, 1772. The 23 year old bride was a widow from Charles City County, Virginia whose father, John Wayles was a lawyer of some renown. After seven pregnancies, and ten years

The signing of the Declaration of Independence.
PAINTING BY JOHN TRUMBULL, COURTESY YALE UNIVERSITY

of marriage, Martha was weakened and died on September 6, 1782. Only two of her children lived to maturity, Martha "Patsy," and Mary "Polly" Jefferson. Distraught by the pending death of his wife, Jefferson promised to never remarry, a promise he kept.

Maria Cosway became a friend of Jefferson after the death of his beloved wife, Martha.
PORTRAIT BY RICHARD COSWAY

Jefferson practiced law until he became a member of the House of Burgesses, where he opposed British control of America. In 1775, he became a member of the Continental Congress and was one of several men assigned to a committee given the task of drafting a declaration of independence. Other members of the committee, Benjamin Franklin, Robert R. Livingston, Roger Sherman and John Adams, believed that Jefferson was the man to sketch out the declaration because of his ability to move people with his powerful writing skills.

Jefferson's daughter, Martha Randolph.
PORTRAIT BY THOMAS SULLY

On June 11, 1776, Jefferson began composing the document that became the cornerstone of American civil rights. His intent was "not to find new principles, or new arguments, never before thought of, not merely to say things which had never been said before; but to place before mankind the common sense of the subject, in terms so plain and firm as to command their assent, and to justify ourselves in the independent stand we are compelled to take...and to give that expression the proper tone and spirit called for by the occasion."

With much congressional discussion and debate, Jefferson's declaration was only amended slightly. When it was finished it read:

"We hold these Truths to be self-evident, that all Men are created equal, that they are endowed by their Creator with certain unalienable rights, that among these are Life, Liberty, and the Pursuit of Happiness– That to secure these Rights, Governments are instituted among Men, deriving their just Powers from the Consent of the Governed, That whenever any Form of Government becomes destructive of these Ends, it is the Right of the People to alter or to abolish it, and to institute new Government, laying its Foundation on such Principles, and organizing its Powers in such Form, as to them shall seem most likely to effect their Safety and Happiness."

Thomas Jefferson
CHARLES W. PEALE

When Jefferson wrote: "All men are created equal," he opened himself up to criticism because he was a slave owner. At the time, at least one-third of the population of Virginia were slaves, and although he tried to effect laws making it easier for Virginians to free their slaves, and lambasted Britain's George III for allowing the "execrable commerce" of slavery, he himself continued to own and profit from the work of slaves. In 1807, President Jefferson was finally able to sign a bill into law banning

Left: The Thomas Jefferson carving on Mount Rushmore was originally placed on Washington's right but was moved to its present position after the granite proved unsuitable for carving.
PHOTO BY RUSS FINLEY

Right: Park Service employees Jeff Glanzer, Karl Bachman and Bob Crisman inspect the Thomas Jefferson sculpture for cracks.
PHOTO BY PAUL HORSTED

the importation of slaves, beginning in 1808.

Jefferson's political career included being a member of the Virginia House of Delegates, from 1776 to 1779, Governor of Virginia, from 1779 to 1781, membership in the Continental Congress from 1783 to 1784, where he helped to create the decimal system. He was Minister to France from 1785 to 1789, and from 1790 to 1793, he was the United State's first Secretary of State. He became vice president during the term of John Adams, when he wrote *A Manual of Parliamentary Practice*, a manual that is still in use in the Senate. He served under Adams from 1797 to 1801, and, in 1801 he was elected President of the United States, serving two consecutive terms.

Perhaps the most momentous achievement of the Jefferson administration was the gigantic land acquisition from France, the Louisiana Purchase, in 1803. He had authorized purchase of New Orleans and West Florida, but Napoleon needed to raise funds for an impending war with Britain, and offered America the Louisiana area for $15 million, or three cents an acre.

Jefferson jumped on the offer and once the Senate ratified the treaty the country's land area doubled. The new American territory consisted of lands

Jefferson at age 78.
PAINTED BY THOMAS SULLY

between the Mississippi River and the Rocky Mountains and included all or part of what is today Louisiana, Arkansas, Iowa, North and South Dakota, Kansas, Nebraska, Missouri, Minnesota, Oklahoma, Texas, New Mexico, Colorado, Wyoming and Montana.

With the Louisiana Purchase came the need to explore the area. Jefferson called upon Meriwether Lewis and William Clark to conduct an expedition. The information brought back by the survey party was invaluable to the expansion of the country.

After his career in politics, Jefferson retired to his Virginia estate, Monticello. Severely in debt, he sold his personal library of 6500 books to the government, effectively founding the Library of Congress after the original library was burned by the British in the War of 1812. His most important accomplishment during his retirement was the creation of the University of Virginia at Charlottesville. Almost every aspect of the development of the college, including

building design, the courses and faculty, were developed by Jefferson. He introduced student electives, allowing students to choose their own classes instead of having to follow a predetermined schedule.

After a long and productive life, President Thomas Jefferson died at Monticello on July 4, 1826, exactly 50 years after the adoption of the Declaration of Independence. Strangely enough, Jefferson's long time friend, fellow signer of the Declaration of Independence and former president, John Adams, also died that day.

Jefferson wrote his own epitaph of: "Here was buried Thomas Jefferson, Author of the Declaration of Independence, of the Statute of Virginia for Religious Freedom, and the Father of the University of Virginia."

"As I would not be a slave, so I would not be a master– This expresses my idea of democracy–Whatever differs from this, to the extent of the differences, is no democracy."
ABRAHAM LINCOLN

P ossibly the most popular president in American History, Abraham Lincoln, born in a log cabin in Hardin (now Larue) County, Kentucky on February 12, 1809, is one of the most beloved American statesmen.

Lincoln's father, Thomas Lincoln, was an illiterate farmer who occasionally worked as a carpenter. His mother, Nancy Hanks Lincoln, died in 1818, leaving 9 year old Abe and his 11 year old sister, Sarah, behind.

A year after his wife's death, Thomas Lincoln married Sarah Bush Johnston, a widow with three children. The loving care and encouragement

Mary Todd Lincoln
MESERVE-KUNHARDT COLLECTION

she showered on young Abraham during childhood would affect him for the rest of his life. In turn, he cared for her deeply. Many years after Lincoln had been assassinated, she was quoted as saying this about her sons, "Both were good boys, but I must say– both now being dead– that Abe was the best boy I ever saw or ever expect to see."

Lincoln's education consisted of little formal schooling. When he learned to read, however, he read everything he could lay his hands

Abraham Lincoln, the 16th U.S. President.

President Jefferson's home, Monticello.

on, and in doing so became self educated.

Before his career in politics, Lincoln worked as a clerk in a general store in New Salem, Illinois. He made $15 a month and slept in the back room. Later, he was part owner of a general store which failed, leaving him responsible for the debt.

He acted as Postmaster of New Salem, earning little money but reading every newspaper that crossed his desk, and also spent time as a surveyor for the county.

His first attempt at politics was an unsuccessful run for state legislature

President Lincoln at General McClellan's headquarters during the Civil War.
COURTESY LIBRARY OF CONGRESS

in 1832. Although he carried New Salem, he came in eighth of 13. He tried again in 1834 and won. He served as Whig floor leader from 1836 until his term ended in 1842. While he was a legislator he studied law and, in 1836, was admitted to the bar.

In 1842, Lincoln married 23 year old Mary Todd. A refined woman who spoke French and studied the arts, Mary was highstrung and emotionally unstable. Pressures caused by her husband's political career exacerbated her men-

tal condition and later in life she was committed for a time to a mental institution.

In 1847, Lincoln became a Congressman, where he opposed American involvement in the Mexican War and worked to abolish slavery in Washington, D.C. He resumed his law career at the end of his term in Congress but was elected to the state legislature in 1854. After his election, he resigned to run for U. S. Senate, but lost to Lyman Trumbull.

In 1858, Lincoln won the Republican Senatorial nomination and gave his famous "House Divided" acceptance speech June 17th, 1858, at the state's Republican convention. He lost the election but would not give up.

Abraham Lincoln in the Great Debate of 1858.
LIBRARY OF CONGRESS

In the 1850s the slavery issue was coming to a head. Southern states felt strongly that they had a right to own slaves, while Northerners believed slavery should be outlawed altogether. Although Lincoln had always believed slavery was wrong, it wasn't until the repeal of the Missouri Compromise, which declared territories outside the south as non-slave areas, that he publicly voiced his opinions. A new Act, called the Kansas and Nebraska Act, determined that people entering the new territories could determine for themselves the issue of slavery in their territories.

Lincoln's speeches earned him attention in his new party, the Republicans. In 1860,

William "Willie" Lincoln is the only child to ever die in the White House.
COURTESY ILLINOIS STATE HISTORICAL LIBRARY, SPRINGFIELD

he was chosen to run for president. Because he had the full support of his party, and the Democrats were splintered, Lincoln became the 16th president of the United States.

He faced a difficult presidency, for shortly after his election the slavery issue finally erupted, and Southern states began to secede from the Union. As predicted by Stephen A. Douglas, "a war of sections, a war of the North against the South, of the free states against the slave states–a war of extermination" was

Far left: President Lincoln at Mount Rushmore.

Left: Geologist Tim Vogt climbs down Lincoln's nose during a study of the monument's cracks.
PHOTOS BY PAUL HORSTED

ahead. The Union was shattering as Jefferson Davis was elected the Confederate president.

On April 12, 1861, the first shots were fired at Fort Sumter, signalling the beginning of the Civil War. The war continued for four long years, until April 9, 1865, when Confederate General Robert E. Lee surrendered to Union General Ulysses S. Grant at Appomattox Courthouse. 624,511 men died during the war, with 475,881 wounded. With the end of the war slavery ended in America.

Five days after the South's defeat, President Lincoln was assassinated by John Wilkes Booth, a Rebel sympathizer. His body lay in state for more than two weeks, and travelled to 14 cities, before being buried in Springfield, Illinois.

Theodore Roosevelt was the 26th president of the United States. He was born in New York City on October 27, 1858, to Theodore Roosevelt, Sr. and Martha Bullock Roosevelt. He would become the youngest person ever to hold the office of the presidency.

A sickly child, he grew up to be an athletic man who was full of energy and filled with wonder at all of nature. He loved animals and thought about a career as a naturalist before he entered politics.

Colonel Theodore Roosevelt and the Rough Riders at San Juan Hill.
HARVARD COLLEGE LIBRARY

Because he was ill as a child, he was educated at home by an aunt, and later by a series of tutors during his early years. As a Harvard student he studied philosophy, German, and science. He graduated magna cum laude in 1880.

Theodore Roosevelt of the Rough Riders.
LIBRARY OF CONGRESS

After a brief stint at Columbia Law School, he dropped out to run for state assemblyman where he served three one year terms, 1882 to 1884, as the youngest member of the assembly of 1882.

On October 27, 1880, Roosevelt married Alice Hathaway Lee, a bright girl of 19, the daughter

Alice Lee Roosevelt
HARVARD COLLEGE LIBRARY

of banker George Cabot Lee. Sadly, the young woman died only four years later from a combination of complications of childbirth and Brights disease. In a tragic turn of events, TR's mother died of typhoid in the same house on

the same day. Roosevelt, feeling depressed and listless, returned to the state assembly and worked like an automaton to keep his mind off of the loss of his wife and mother. During this time he crossed party lines to support Grover Cleveland for president and sponsored the civil service reform act.

From 1884 until 1886, he lived in the Dakota Territory where he ran a cattle ranch and was deputy sheriff of Billings County.

Roosevelt married Edith Kermit Carow on December 2, 1886, in London. She was a longtime friend and neighbor of TR's and had been a guest at his first wedding. Their marriage was strong and produced five children; Theodore Jr., Kermit, Ethel, Archibald and Quentin.

He became president of the New York City Police Board in 1895, and worked vigorously to clean up the notoriously corrupt Police Department. His service to this department gained him national attention.

In 1897, he was appointed assistant secretary of the Navy where his energy and enthusiasm were boundless. One of his ideas was the use of airplanes for military purposes.

A member of the National Guard, Roosevelt was commander of a volunteer cavalry known

as the Rough Riders, who served at Las Guásimas, Cuba. Roosevelt became famous for his heroic charge up San Juan Hill where he and his men met the enemy in combat. It was reported by Major General Leonard Wood, that Roosevelt was first to reach the enemy trenches where he killed an enemy soldier with his bare hands. He was promoted to colonel for his acts of bravery.

As Governor of New York, from 1898 to 1900, he was talked into running for vice president in 1900. He was nominated with 925 out of 926 possible votes. He became president September 14th, 1901, when President McKinley died by an assassin's bullet.

Edith Carow Roosevelt was TR's second wife.
LIBRARY OF CONGRESS

Roosevelt's greatest accomplishments were building the Panama Canal, negotiating the Treaty of Portsmouth, breaking apart monopolies, his advocacy of labor and consumer rights and the conservation of 125 million acres in national forest lands.

Right: Theodore Roosevelt carving, July 4, 1989.
PHOTO BY PAUL HORSTED

Below: A mountain goat stares up at the carving of Theodore Roosevelt on Mount Rushmore.
PHOTO BY PAUL HORSTED

Back cover: Mount Rushmore National Memorial.
PHOTO BY RUSS FINLEY